WHY INTERNET PORN MATTERS

T0355772

WHY INTERNET PORN MATTERS

MARGRET GREBOWICZ

stanford briefs
An Imprint of Stanford University Press
Stanford, California

Stanford University Press
Stanford, California

©2013 by the Board of Trustees of the
Leland Stanford Junior University.
All rights reserved.

Printed and bound by CPI Group (UK) Ltd,
Croydon, CR0 4YY

Library of Congress Cataloging-in-Publication Data

Grebowicz, Margret, 1973– author.
  Why internet porn matters / Margret Grebowicz.
    pages cm
  Includes bibliographical references.
  ISBN 978-0-8047-8662-1 (pbk. : alk. paper)
  1. Internet pornography—Philosophy. 2. Pornography—
Political aspects. 3. Feminist theory. I. Title.
  HQ471.G735 2013
  363.4'702854678—dc23   2012043691

  ISBN 978-0-8047-8670-6 (electronic)

Typeset by Classic Typography in 10/13 Adobe Garamond

THE OBSESSIVE FEAR OF THE
AMERICANS IS THAT THE LIGHTS
MIGHT GO OUT.

—JEAN BAUDRILLARD

CONTENTS

ACKNOWLEDGMENTS

A special thanks goes to Johanna Oksala for suggesting that I turn a conference paper into this book, and for inviting me to write it in residence at the University of Dundee. Thanks to the Dundee philosophy department, as well as Paul Bowman, Michael Goddard, Lynn Turner, Mohammed Abed, Peter Gratton, Eduardo Mendieta, and Anne O'Byrne, for inviting me to present the research in its earliest forms at their respective universities. Thanks also to colleagues Marguerite Hoyt, Ann Cahill, Karmen MacKendrick, Amy Allen, Noelle McAffee, Nsenga Burton, and three anonymous reviewers for posing just the right questions and directing me to new texts, and to my philosophy colleagues at Goucher College for supporting my extended leave. Support for research and writing time was provided by Goucher College, The Leverhulme Trust, and The University of Dundee.

Support for my spirit was provided by the loved ones, collaborators, muses, jokesters, sages, minxes, and sphinxes who offered enthusiasm for and relief from this project as I labored: Lee Lawson, Brian Moretta, Julie Milgram, Jacquelyn Schlossman, Max Lents, Lia Litosseliti, Ewa Skowska, William Tatge, Ben Monder, Rich Woodson, Josh Roseman, Janusz Grebowicz, David Carr, Kirby, Maciej Grebowicz, Mark Ferber, and my students, especially (but not only) those in Philosophical Topics: Pornography in the fall of 2012.

WHY INTERNET PORN MATTERS

1 THE CRITICAL LANDSCAPE OF PORNOGRAPHY

WHY INTERNET PORN
SHOULD MATTER TO PHILOSOPHERS

Given the number of different discourses and methodologies with which it is possible to define, examine, and evaluate pornography today, there is surprisingly little philosophical theorizing about it. There is certainly no shortage of feminist legal and sociological literature about the effects of pornography on women's lives and psyches and on the production of gender. The spectrum of positions extends from the most "anti-," through arguments that the industry is work like any other work, into arguments that pornography functions as a political speech and thus is not like any other work but a site of resistance, even a creative avenue for reclaiming the body and rescripting sexual practices. Recently, the emerging field of porn theory has successfully motivated the study of pornography as a form of culture. However, even as topics like sexual difference, objectification, and spectacle take on a life beyond feminist theory, and subjects like technology, capitalism, and the democratization of information do so beyond critical theory, philosophers have been slow to turn their attention to pornography, the largest and fastest growing commodity on the "information superhighway."

To begin, then, and if I may be allowed a tenuous distinction for the sake of making a point, this is a work of philosophy before it is a work of feminist theory. In the tradition of Foucault's *History of Sexuality, Volume 1*, a philosophical examination of sexuality, subjectivity, and knowledge, which was only later appropriated and put to good use by feminist thinkers, I make an argument concerning pornography's role in political ontology that is appropriable not just for feminist concerns but for critical social projects in general. I aim to show that turning to the philosophical register results in reorienting what might be called the politics of pornography. The feminist contribution so far may be summarized as the successful shifting of the debate from problems of censorship and freedom of speech to questions of gender, and particularly gender understood as power difference. I here argue that the intersection of pornography and Internet distribution effects yet another shift in what pornography means and how it functions in the world. Internet distribution is not merely a new, faster delivery method that results in nothing more than more and more porn. The Internet fundamentally changes the social meaning of pornography by embedding it squarely in the epistemological shift from knowledge to information, and the political shift to information becoming democratically accessible to everyone. These shifts, in which Internet pornography acts as a catalyst, effect a noninnocent, particular understanding of the sexual subject in relationship to the democratic state and to speech, one which, I argue, constrains the possibilities for sexual speech, pornographic or otherwise, to resist or intervene in the state's policies. To borrow Foucault's term, Internet pornography creates unprecedentedly docile subjects. At stake is the governability of the embodied subject that presents as simultaneously sexual and speaking.

My attunement to the philosophical register should not be read within an academic hierarchy in which philosophy and other "old school," "boy's club" disciplines take priority over feminist theory.

It is a methodological decision in direct response to the sea of questions I encountered in the course of presenting my work. The one that consistently returned was *What is to be done about pornography?* As this book makes clear, a philosophical approach does not propose to answer this question. In fact, there are many aspects of pornography that cannot be properly, robustly discussed in the philosophical register. Some are more obvious than others. For instance, this approach does not yield statistics or interpret them. It does not have much to say about the demographics of pornography consumption or production, or about the psychophysical complexities of the experience of moving images, or about the market for French Catholic nun pornography in eighteenth-century England, or about the long-term economic effects of file sharing on the commercial pornography market, as opposed to the amateur market. It deliberately avoids the discourse of addiction, largely because I do not know how to think about addiction without relying on a framework of norms and pathologies, with its attendant ontological assumptions about autonomy, dependency, self-control, values—all of which are necessarily thrown into crisis by the thinking of the event and the inhuman that I invoke in my argument. It is ambivalent about the category of desire, because this category remains inextricably bound to psychoanalysis and the concepts and methods proper to it. A psychoanalytic approach to Internet pornography would be relevant and timely, but it is not the one I offer here, even as I gesture, somewhat obliquely, towards categories like fantasy and abjectitude. Porn theorist Laura Kipnis writes that pornography is interesting to talk about precisely because there is so much more at stake than just sexual pleasure, and the above are just a few examples of the possible alternative directions for analyzing this "more" (1999, 201).

But the philosophical offers critical trajectories that no other register does. Although it is easy to make the case that thinking and writing about pornography requires an interdisciplinary approach, combining resources from visual studies, cultural studies, feminist theory, economics, media studies, political science, and history, I contend that certain discipline-specific questions should be prioritized. The case for interdisciplinarity tends to be made in any analysis of popular culture, and it could be argued that the philosophical register is the one most "allergic" to this kind of work. But how can we propose to examine pornography without considering the weight of the following: What is freedom? What are norms? What does it mean to be embodied? What does it mean to be a speaking subject? What makes something "sexual"? And then there is the normative aspect of what philosophers do, which results in questions not about what is, but what should be. What should be the role of the state in the production of sexualities? What is the best way to conceive of rights in liberationist projects? Should we attempt to define pornography or not, and what is to be gained (and by whom) from either approach? This is not to say that the feminist insight that gender is a power differential should no longer be important for those of us working on pornography. That would be a ridiculous claim. Neither is it to say that critically examining the contents of pornography is not important work. It is simply to indicate that a trajectory has been overlooked and should be incorporated into our discussions of this issue, which has been so hotly contested by feminists for the past four decades. There are many glaring, important issues that this book deliberately does not explore—for instance, how race functions in pornography—only because in my research I did not find them fundamentally changed in response to the technology of Internet distribution.

There are also philosophers appearing only in the peripheries of this book—most notably, Luce Irigaray—whose work offers important contributions to the pornography debate but does not engage with the role of technologies in the formation of subjectivities directly enough to help us interrogate the intersection of pornography and the Internet. My trajectory requires moving from discussing the contents of pornography to discussing something like its form, those structural and logical particularities which allow it to play a pivotal role in the democratization of information. My main critical paradigm for this is Jean Baudrillard's development of the idea he calls "America" in his book by the same title. In Catharine MacKinnon and Andrea Dworkin's analysis of the social meanings and political effects of commercial pornography, a polemical and aggressive critique that has been championed, caricatured, misread, rejected, and reanimated by feminist thinkers since its appearance, we encounter the claim that pornography is symptomatic of America.[1] Starting from this and following Baudrillard, I argue that Internet pornography is symptomatic of and central to a kind of modernity that may be called "American" in its particular production of governable subjects. My claims will not concern the United States as a concrete pornography market, but America (or what Dworkin calls "Amerika") as an imaginary. This book presents a poststructuralist critique of the politics of the First Amendment and their central role in the formation of this imaginary, interrogating the relationships between speech, freedom, sexuality, and power as they are produced and maintained by the commodification of information, as well as the effect of the dematerialization of commodities on the idea of the real.

DEFINITIONS, DEBATES, AND CRITICAL PARADIGMS

To begin with the most obvious of philosophical questions, what is pornography? The problem of definition is well known and often invoked as part of the argument against the legal repression of pornographic materials. If we decide to censor, the worry goes, what will be the fate of works by artists such as Robert Mapplethorpe and Norman Mailer? What should be done about ad campaigns like those of Victoria's Secret, which openly draw on soft-core tropes, and American Apparel, which invoke the semiotics of amateur "teen" hard-core sites? Won't we have to censor more things than necessary? I encounter this question from the audience every time I present my research: what do you do about the fact that pornography is so difficult to define and circumscribe? If it is impossible to point to exactly what makes something pornographic, then how is that elusive thing to be theoretically examined, much less politically acted upon?

Harriet Gilbert writes that "the recent obsession with a definition—especially with a foolproof, clear-cut, legal definition—has not only distracted from but positively harmed understanding" in the debates concerning pornography (1992, 217). Is it possible to understand the phenomenon of pornography without arriving at a definition of it? Arguably, definition must precede analysis, so that, at the very least, we all know what we're talking about. Equally arguably, however, the reason pornography remains such a complex and daunting topic that it demands ever more analysis is precisely that it is so difficult to define. The p-word is loaded, to put it mildly.[2] Gilbert advocates suspending the use of the word and discussing instead something like literatures of sex, a category in which the stuff that is easily recognizable as pornography would commingle with art and other cultural production in which explicit sexuality poses some degree of threat to personal boundaries and the social order. It is this broader phenomenon that we should be trying to understand, she argues, rather than looking for ways to define the pornographic so that we may then affect it legally, whether by posing constraints or protections. Linda Williams also argues against a stable definition, beginning from the position that what we call "pornography" is actually an irreducible plurality of pornographies, a diffuse and complex family of phenomena to be treated as such, and that the question of its political belonging (on which so much feminist intellectual energy is spent) is only one of many theoretical problems posed by the existence of pornographies.

I agree with both Gilbert and Williams to a certain degree. However, as someone for whom the question of political belonging remains pressing, I will continue to use the word *pornography* and to use it in the singular for strategic reasons. While I concur with Williams that "there is no monolithic pathology that can be demonized as obscene pornography" but instead there are only irreducibly plural and multivalent pornographies, within the boundaries of that claim it remains necessary to account for what one means by the word (1992, 264). I also take issue with Williams's claim that the question of pornography's political belonging, for which I will use the shorthand question *Is pornography part of the problem or part of the solution?* is merely one question among others. I contend that in the case of Internet pornography, the question of political belonging must be foregrounded. The shift from previous forms of distribution to the Internet forces us to consider the central role of contemporary pornography in the changing dynamics between sexual freedom and freedom of expression, as well as fantasy and social change.

All disclaimers aside, then, what is pornography? I have two answers to this, one literal and simple, and the other more complex. The first concerns specifically what I mean by "Internet porn" in the present study, namely materials created specifically to aid in masturbation and circulated on the Internet, largely (though not exclusively) for commercial purposes. I am not interested in a clear-cut legal definition but in one which will allow me to get on with the project of thinking critically about a cultural phenomenon, or at the very least a set of materials and a set of practices. The question for me concerns not what people are actually masturbating to, but what has been created specifically for that purpose. Someone may indeed masturbate while reading *Lolita*, but that is an issue for a different study. The pornography subgenre "lolicon" (short for "Lolita complex"), however, a kind of cartoon imagery depicting very young girls with infantlike bodies penetrated by penises, fingers, and sometimes monster tentacles, has been created specifically and exclusively to sexually arouse to the point of orgasm. Lolicon, not *Lolita*, is what I mean by "pornography." Likewise, the fact that someone somewhere may be masturbating to veterinary photographs of cow genitalia is not my concern. My concern is directed at a website like petsex.com, a bestiality pornography site, which features among other things films of farm animals mating. These were originally filmed for some other purpose but are placed on this site explicitly and deliberately packaged as pornography, edited and presented specifically for fans of bestiality sites to masturbate to. This kind of packaging and presentation of preexisting materials counts as "creating" pornography in my study.

As the example above illustrates, it is always possible to cite an image, from which it follows that it is equally possible to extract pornographic imagery like the aforementioned loli manga and present it in a different context, as artists sometimes do. This maintains the familiar controversy concerning the relationship of pornography to art (*Is it pornography? Is it art? Can art be pornographic, and vice versa?*). In the case of Mapplethorpe and Sade, for instance, the answer is clearly yes: artworks and pornography are not necessarily mutually exclusive. But the fact that the context of consumption is this important in determining whether the contents of the materials are properly pornographic simply underlines the point I will attempt to show: that in the phrase "Internet porn" the former word is at least as significant as the latter. In other words, in the age of Internet distribution, whatever question we ask about pornography's social effects and political significance cannot be answered without taking the mode of distribution into account.

On one hand, then, the question of definition is simply not that important except for practical or strategic purposes, so that we may agree, however temporarily, on what it is we are discussing with the aim of continuing the discussion. On the other hand, any serious theoretical encounter with pornography—including methodology, the particular shape of the inquiry, and something like a "position" vis-à-vis a politically divisive and inflammatory cultural phenomenon—depends precisely on stability of definition or, rather, on making a compelling case that pornography is better conceived of as *this kind of thing rather than another*. But this is a different meaning of the word *is*, one less concerned with delimiting a certain range of materials and more concerned with what we might call the ontology of pornography.

The political belonging of pornography is intimately linked to its ontology: any answer to *Is pornography part of the problem or part of the solution?* is in a coconstitutive relationship to any answer to *What kind of thing is pornography?* MacKinnon and Dworkin knew this when they first proposed that pornography is not speech, in an effort to dislodge it from anxieties about state infringement on First Amendment rights (see MacKinnon 1987, 149). If pornography could no longer be defined as speech, then it could not be protected under the constitutional right to free speech. MacKinnon and Dworkin could not have made as forceful, far-reaching, and controversial a critique as they did had they not essentially rebooted the debate on the ontological level, beginning with the proposal that we think of pornography as a different kind of thing. Most of the work done on pornography today refers obligingly (and almost always very critically, even dismissively) to them as pioneers of the antiporn position.

However, as historian Matthew Lasar shows, debates about pornography have a long and rich history prior to the feminist critiques, including the argument, "well established by the 1870's, that pornographic representations cause people to commit acts of violence" (1995, 182). What makes the feminist contributions to the pornography debates so innovative that they quickly overshadow previous—and ongoing—arguments by conservatives and civil libertarians is that they "unquestionably revolutionized *how we think about* pornography," causing tectonic shifts on the ontological level (182, emphasis added). MacKinnon and Dworkin argued that pornography depicts not ideas, much less fantasies, but real events happening to real people. Unlike earlier periods when erotica and pornography flourished, like the sixteenth century in Italy and the eighteenth in England, in contemporary pornography the sex is not fantasized—someone is actually performing it as it is being filmed or photographed (see MacKinnon 1993a). This, they argued, necessarily changes the terms of the debate from problems of speech and civil liberties to problems of practice and power.

Accordingly, much of the work written explicitly against Mac-Kinnon and Dworkin, most notably by Ronald Dworkin and Nadine Strossen, attempts precisely to reverse this movement, rearticulating the stakes in terms of speech, ideas, and freedom of expression, in particular political expression. I will not detail the speech-versus-practice debate here, because Joan Mason-Grant already does this very well in the introduction to her book *Pornography Embodied: From Speech to Sexual Practice*. Indeed, more recent books like Mason-Grant's and Pamela Paul's *Pornified* respond to the cyberlibertarian move to rearticulate pornography in terms of speech by, again, insisting on the advantages of the practice paradigm. And so the back-and-forth between the two ontologies continues.

Mason-Grant articulates the practice paradigm differently and more efficiently, in some ways, than MacKinnon and Dworkin. Where they argued that pornography depicts not ideas but practices, Mason-Grant develops a theory of the consumption of pornography as itself a practice. In other words, she shifts the critique from the material reality of the sex acts being filmed to the material reality of the sex act that is the use of pornography. Phenomenological analysis allows her to further the MacKinnon/Dworkin position in more complex terms by showing use in particular to be embodied, material practice. "Regarding the question of consumption," she writes, "the use of pornographic materials in sex is not best conceptualized on the model of representations that are contemplated, scrutinized, and evaluated. Rather, they are used, enacted, performed, acted out, and rehearsed in real life in socially constructed, irreducibly embodied activities" (33).

She goes on to extend MacKinnon and Dworkin's critique by showing how the use of pornography comes to have subordinating effects in practice. MacKinnon and Dworkin reorient the debate concerning pornography as an issue of power from the power of the state over the private individual to the power of one social group (men) over another (women). However, this leaves them open to critiques such as Amy Allen's, who argues that their position depends on too reductive a definition of power as limited to relations of domination and subordination, when in fact different definitions of power are possible and even appropriate to discussions of pornography (2001). Mason-Grant's analysis avoids this criticism. She writes,

> The sexual dynamic in mainstream pornography is one of overt or implied struggle—involving either flight and capture or, more subtly, resistance and subduing and possession. The resolution of the sexual tension, the closing act of the performance, is male ejaculation, the male spent and satisfied. These are the regulative norms of mainstream pornography, and they create what counts as normal and perverse, sexy and asexual, identifying the paths of access to social viability as a sexual actor. In the account of the social practice I have elaborated here, they do not function primarily as ideas that we contemplate and over which we engage in explicit and critical debate. Rather, they are enacted—acted out—in sexual practice. . . . To use misogynist, heterosexist, racist, . . . pornography routinely is *repetitively* to experience these social relations of domination and subordination through sexual arousal and pleasure, and, conversely, *repetitively* to experience sexual arousal and pleasure through these social relations. (129)

In other words, insofar as much mainstream pornography overtly depicts subordination and dominance, the material practice of pornography allows the body to experience intense pleasure at these social relations. The problem is not that pornography somehow magically, automatically grants men power over women, or even, *pace* MacKinnon and Dworkin, that the men in pornography exercise real power over the women with whom they have sex, but that men consuming pornography experience physical pleasure at the sights and sounds of the subordination of women.

From here, however, it is still a far leap to showing how relations of domination and subordination function to shut down *speech* in particular. As Mason-Grant argues that pornography is best understood as a sexual practice which codes subordination as bodily pleasure and has material effects on women as a group, effects which then in turn compromise speech, she remains unable to show that pornography is any different from any other (subordinating) sexual practice in this respect. Similar arguments using notions like norms, repetition, and "paths of access to social viability" may be made about nonpornographic, real-life sex, and certainly about rape or for that matter any other material practice of subordination (battery, harassment) operative in silencing those who are being subordinated. In fact, at the heart of MacKinnon's analysis of patriarchy is the idea that domination is prior to gender difference and that heterosexual relations are at their very core relations of domination and subordination. On this model, pornography is just another heterosexual practice, holding no special place except perhaps as a sort of user's manual. What remains to be shown is that pornography has *unique* effects on the capacity to speak, and that it is for this reason that it deserves particular attention from feminist and other liberationist projects. For the practice paradigm, the relationships among pornography (as opposed to sex in general), speech, and freedom remain to be convincingly worked out.

On the propornography or "sex radical" side of the debate, there are multiple takes on the role of pornography in heterosexual practice. Gayle Rubin, for instance, harbors the same assumption as the antipornography positions when writing that "a woman who enjoys pornography (even if that means enjoying a rape fantasy) is in a sense a rebel, insisting on an aspect of her sexuality that has been defined as a male preserve" (1992, 278). The assumption is that Western culture represses sexuality, particularly women's sexuality, and women who embrace pornography are embracing their sexuality. There are other, in my opinion more significant defenses of pornography which depend on an original *dis*junction between pornography and other sexual practices. While, in the practice paradigm, the claim that pornography normalizes misogynistic sex ends up essentially collapsing the distinction between pornography and the rest of sexual practice, this more nuanced propornography position counters the normalizing schema by unhooking pornography from the rest of sex. In other words, pornography cannot be conceived as a user's manual in any straightforward way. For example, Williams argues against the notion that pornography normalizes heterosexist, misogynistic practices by showing that, by means of various conventions, it positions the viewer as a "pervert" and his or her pleasure as perverse. The persistent demand for pornography (as distinct from the demand for sex) functions as proof that no sexuality is normal, that "a perverse dynamic operates in all forms of sexual fantasy; . . . it is inevitable both within heterosexual pornography and outside it. . . . This idea of perversion is important to the agency and empowerment of those non-dominant, minority sexualities frequently condemned as perverse and evident in gay, lesbian, sadomasochistic and bisexual pornography" (1992, 243). The value of pornography, then, extends far beyond simple use to the queering of all sexuality, showing, against heterosexist normalization, that "we are all perverts in our desires" (264).

In a book on the other side of the spectrum from Mason-Grant's, Laura Kipnis's *Bound and Gagged: Pornography and the Politics of Fantasy in America* urges us to begin from the assumption that pornography is at least as complex and sophisticated as any other pop culture. Even more than the other forms, pornography tells the truth about the culture that produces it:

> As the avant-garde knew, transgression is no simple thing: it's a precisely calculated cultural endeavor. It means knowing the culture inside and out, discerning its secret shames and grubby secrets, and

knowing how to best humiliate it, knock it off its prim perch. . . .
A culture's pornography becomes, in effect, a very precise map of that
culture's borders: pornography begins at the edge of that culture's
decorum. Carefully tracing that edge, like an anthropologist mapping
a culture's system of taboos and myths, gives you a detailed blueprint
of the culture's anxieties, investments, contradictions. (164)

Williams and Kipnis argue that pornography does not normalize
anything but instead queers sexuality and transgresses norms,
exposing their contingency and limits. Thus, even this work,
which does a better job of treating pornography as "its own thing"
and not as just one piece of the larger puzzle of sex, still ultimately
values pornography in terms of the sexual practices beyond it,
locating it in queer and nonnormative sexualities in general.

Of both these "camps," it is Mason-Grant who limits her analysis to a particular kind of pornography, namely mainstream heterosexual hard core. While Williams and Kipnis describe all
pornography as complex, transgressive, and denormalizing,
Mason-Grant limits her claims to the mainstream, on which she
focuses her argument that it normalizes subordination. She leaves
open the possibility for other subgenres to be socially progressive.
Williams and Kipnis, on the other hand, ascribe the same political
meaning to all contemporary pornography and argue for its cultural and political value across the board. This metalevel difference
between the arguments is not an accident, since Williams and
Kipnis, whom we might call the "revolutionary fantasists," make
claims about something like a "pornographic imagination" in general and its function in relationship to power. And it is precisely
this that interests me, which is why I too will deliberately refer to
a monolithic pornography.

None of the positions I have detailed here offer satisfactory
accounts of the relationships among pornography, speech, and
something like "freedom." Williams will not go as far as to argue
that pornography can or does serve a liberatory function in general, but only to make the historical point that the legalization of

pornography has served that function, opening the door to more queer pornographies, which she takes to be a specific form of resistance to straight, misogynistic mainstream pornography. "It is because moving-image pornography became legal in the USA that the once off-scene voices of women, gays, lesbians, sadomasochists, and bisexuals have been heard opposing and negating the heterosexual, males-only pornography that once dominated" (1992, 262–63).

Kipnis claims that there are important *political* reasons to read pornography as something akin to fiction. She argues that our failure to see pornography as a medium for fiction and fantasy is politically dangerous, especially from the vantage point of the feminist demand for new futures, sexualities, and subjectivities. Pornography is "both a legitimate form of culture and a fictional, fantastical, even allegorical realm; it neither simply reflects the real world nor is it some hypnotizing call to action" (163). The last sentence could be directed at projects like Mason-Grant's, which try to account for precisely the ties between pornography, the real, and action, though no one reading her analysis will walk away thinking that the reflection is "simple" or that the norms function by "hypnotizing" anyone. As convincingly as Kipnis shows that pornography is not these things, she does not tell us much about what it *is*. More precisely, she goes only as far as to show that pornography is best conceived and analyzed as the complex phenomenon called "fantasy," but she stops short of exploring how fantasy acts in the world, what it "does," as it were, beyond its effect on the psyche of the individual subject.

2 WHY SPEECH STILL MATTERS

THE PROBLEM OF SPEECH

In one sense feminist projects that direct us away from the speech paradigm are absolutely right to do so, because, as I will show, the paradigm has operated with the wrong model of speech. Speech has traditionally been assumed to be the direct expression of "ideas that we contemplate and over which we engage in explicit and critical debate" (Mason-Grant), or as "simply reflect[ing] the real world" (Kipnis). One response to this error has come from philosophy of language, where speech act theorists, working with a model of language in which certain utterances "do" things in the world or effect states of affairs, debate the possibilities for pornography to actually do the things MacKinnon and Dworkin claim it does: subordinate and silence women.[1] But their own work gets bogged down in rather technical discussions of speech act theory itself, with which I will not engage here. I am concerned with a different sense in which language does things in the world, namely the way that the changes in porno*graphy* not only reflect but effect shifts in the social imaginary in which sexualities, speech, and freedom intersect.

Furthermore, what I am calling "the problem of speech," the knot of complex relations between sex, speech, and power, remains implicit in feminist debates even after the speech paradigm is explicitly abandoned. We see this in the ways that personal testimony, both central to and contested throughout the pornography debates, causes ongoing conceptual trouble. According to Carol Smart, the function of testimony must be examined because it reinscribes a moral dimension in a debate that has historically disassociated itself from any discourse about morality. "It is as if we have come to assume that whenever a feminist speaks, what comes out is politics, not morals, no matter what she is saying. The distinction between politics and morality has absolved us of the need to be rigorous about moral issues, because morality was seen as a diversion and merely a question on the reactionaries' agenda" (1992, 187). However, Smart points out, moral claims are constantly smuggled back into the pornography debate, as the latter remains set up as a war between two sides with different rhetorical strategies. For Smart, the most problematic rhetorical strategy is the use of first-person testimonies by women, which, she says, have been at the center of the "pro-censorship lobby" (see MacKinnon 1993a). "The way in which the argument has been structured allows of only two positions: anti-porn/pro-censorship and pro-porn/anti-censorship. This binary dichotomy locates the moral high ground with the pro-censorship lobby" when the latter introduces testimony by porn workers or women affected by pornography in other ways, testimonies which detail abuse, imprisonment, rape, and so on. "In this formulation good can easily be distinguished from evil" (Smart, 196).

Robert Jensen makes this move, adding the testimonies of men who use pornography to those of women who describe the sexual abuse they have suffered in terms of connections to consumption. Jensen argues for the narrative approach in epistemological and methodological terms: "The search for causation demands 'science,' while a concern for pornography's role in rape leaves us open to listening to stories. . . . A shift in emphasis and method offers a way to state not The Truth (or to conclude that we do not yet know The Truth), but a way to tell true stories and begin to make trustworthy moral and political decisions" (1998, 101). Jensen then goes on to present narratives by women from various social scientific studies of pornography and to add numerous narratives by men—porn users, convicted sex offenders, as well as himself as a child and adult consumer of porn. And yet the rhetoric of the value of narrative changes as his analysis moves from female (victim) speakers to male (perpetrator) speakers. The value of listening to the male narratives is presented in epistemological and methodological terms, not unlike Pamela Paul's claim that the value of conducting numerous interviews of people "expressly chosen to provide a broad spectrum" lies in the possibility of reconstructing a "profile" of the pornography user (2005, 10–11). The point of Paul's interviews and Jensen's male narratives is the value of "real-life experiences" for representation of a certain type, namely the porn consumer. In contrast, Jensen's justification of his use of personal narratives by women is noticeably morally laden. What feminist in his or her right mind would dare contest that "we desperately need . . . to listen to these women, to acknowledge that their experiences are real, to acknowledge that they are real and that they matter"? (1998, 119). Smart argues that

> this form of argument, which might otherwise be transparent, is protected when used in conjunction with the personal testimony. For by opposing it in this context one is effectively placed in the position of speaking not against a relatively powerful woman like MacKinnon [or a relatively powerful man like Jensen], but against less well-resourced women who have given testimony of abuse. Thus one appears to be denying their experience, or suggesting that it is of no consequence. . . . This is a particular dilemma for feminists. (190)

Indeed, what kind of role personal testimony should play in critical feminist discourse has posed a dilemma for feminists in all areas, as we reflect on questions of epistemic authority (whose voice counts as feminist?), the contested nature of the very idea of "women's experience" (is there such a thing?), and power differences among women (who has access to speech, and how is that access mediated?). Shannon Bell's groundbreaking book *Reading, Writing, and Rewriting the Prostitute Body* takes on precisely these questions as she creates a textual encounter between the voices of prostitutes (she prefers this term to *sex workers*) and those of feminist theorists. Bell theorizes prostitute testimonies as presented in their performance art in order to include their experiences and perspectives in debates about pornography and prostitution. "The aim is to present their work as little narratives that function to intervene in larger hegemonic, feminist, and even prostitute discourses," precisely because these discourses, particularly feminism, have traditionally denied speech to what Bell calls "pornographic women" (1994, 137). Prior to any question of the contents of the speech, what is important to Bell about performance art by artist-activists like Annie Sprinkle is that it "presents a particular female body, the body that dominant discourse and feminist discourse have marked as the obscene, the other, from the position of this body—speaking" (142). Bell's commitment to hearing prostituted women speak for themselves is not simply due to her curiosity about what they will say. It is at the center of her methodology and argument that feminist representations of prostitutes have in fact systematically distorted the truth of those experiences.

The two points in which I am interested are the importance Bell places on showing the prostitutes as speaking "for themselves," and the idea that their speech "intervenes" in dominant discourse. The latter point is political, and I will return to it later. The former point is vulnerable to Smart's critique of MacKinnon. By introducing testimony that is *valuable qua testimony* (prior to examining the contents), Bell effectively sneaks in a moral criticism of anyone who questions the kind of theory that Bell then "extracts" or grafts onto the prostitute testimonies. To paraphrase Smart, one appears then to speak not against a relatively powerful woman (Dr. Shannon Bell) but the less-resourced women she presents in her work, which returns us to the problem of how to face the "dilemma" that testimony poses for feminism. *Pace* Smart, the moral high ground is deployed not just by the procensorship side but by any position that obligates one to listen to the voices of women that are otherwise being silenced.

It appears that we cannot escape questions of speech—what it is, how it works, how it acts on the world—even, or perhaps particularly, in discussing pornography. Although Bell never once invokes any notion of "free speech," the first point brings her close to Strossen's critique of cyberpuritanism, which may not be all that surprising in the end, given that both thinkers identify as pornography defenders. Strossen fears that the repression of sexual expression does most political harm to the very minorities that feminism seeks to liberate—women and sexual orientation minorities—as it shuts down expression of their "true" sexualities (2000, xix). This is related to the criticism so commonly wielded against MacKinnon that it's become canonical: that her critique of the cultural meanings of heterosexual sex does not allow for women's sexual agency (see for instance Bell, 83). At stake for both Strossen's cyberlibertarianism and Bell's porn-positivity is the connection between sexual agency and speech, and both argue that as some feminisms shut down one, they shut down the other, and for precisely those social groups suffering under patriarchy.

As a First Amendment defender, Strossen works with a model of speech in which a natural speech preexists the "hegemonic" or "dominant" discourses, or in Strossen's account, "the state," which in turn either get in the way of speech or stay out of its way. In Strossen's use of the phrase "sexual expression" throughout her book, "expression" implies the externalizing of something that was there before the expression, an idea or some other kind of interior event, and the suppression of this externalizing amounts to a forcible keeping-in of something that wants out. This pathological and particularly American-puritanical repression of speech is coextensive with the repression of sexualities, which were also there "before" the repressive regimes. Strossen recognizes (xiv–xv) that the imperative to "protect" speech is also particularly American, part of the neoliberal logic of a state whose legal code centers on a Bill of Rights; but despite making the imperative historically located and contingent, she never really questions the idea that it is always best to speak, to express, to externalize.[2]

But this is not the only way to conceive of speech or expression and its relationship to agency. In her analysis of the logic of confession, Judith Butler illustrates another possibility: "The point is not to ferret out desires and expose their truth in public, but rather to constitute a truth of oneself through the act of verbalization itself. The first relies on a repressive hypothesis; the second emphasizes instead the performative force of spoken utterance" (2004b, 163). Butler focuses on the ways in which confession is not archaeological, unearthing something hidden, but productive of something new. The role of the listener/interpreter is "not to discern a preexisting truth but to facilitate a detachment of the self from itself" so that this self becomes subject to interpretation (164). "The self in its priority is not being discovered in such a moment, but becoming elaborated, through speaking, in a new way, in the course of conversation" (173). Bell's project of making prostitute performances audible to and relevant for academic feminism is better understood in Butler's terms: the value of speech in this case is not that it releases something repressed but that it allows for the dynamic, ongoing elaboration of a self. This means understanding speech as in some sense constitutive of the self, an idea in circulation in feminist discourse since Foucault's critique of the repressive hypothesis, which Butler in fact follows in her account of confessional speech.

Any attempt to wrest discussions of pornography away from questions of speech may be taken to overlook Foucault's crucial insights in the *History of Sexuality, Volume 1*, namely that sex, discourse, power, and knowledge are inextricably linked and that this linkage is symptomatic of modernity. Foucault's notion of biopower shows that sexuality is regulated not by power repressing it from above but by normalizing discourses and the disciplining of bodies, all of which functions not just as constraint but in fact productively. On this account, sexuality, understood as a discursive effect, is where power "lives." Thus, any possibility of resistance must have the body as its proper site, and this body must somehow resist the discourses which shape sex, discourses like medicine, science, criminology, psychology, and so on.

According to Johanna Oksala (2005), in Foucault's later work, pleasure, as opposed to desire, is the possibility of freedom. "While modern techniques of power use desire to attach to us a true self defined in part by our sexuality, the notion of pleasure cannot be used in the same way as a tool for social and scientific regulation. The sexual body understood as a body experiencing pleasure and not as a determinable object of the sciences and of institutional practices becomes a possibility of subverting normalization" (129). Oksala argues that sex understood as a limit experience offers the same possibility:

> There are experiences that fall outside of what is constituted by discourse in the sense that these abject or transgressive experiences are rendered mute and unintelligible in our culture. . . . The sexual body as experiencing is capable of multiplying, distorting, and overflowing its discursive definitions, classifications and coordinates. The experiential body can take normal language to the point where it fails, where it loses its power of definition, or even of expression. . . . The experience of the limit can be realized in language but only at the moment "where it says what cannot be said." (130)

Thus, it would seem, insofar as pornography is involved in the production of pleasure and is itself, as Mason-Grant argues so well, a form of sexual experience and not just sexual discourse, it could be related to freedom somehow.

But what about pornography as discourse and not experience? How does the idea of porn as part of the discursive production of sexual practices relate to Foucault's claim about the limits of language? What about "speaking sex," the *graphe* of the pornographic: when is that normative, when is it resistant, and how can we tell the difference? The idea that discourse is constitutive of subjectivity, operative in both Bell and Butler, does not suffice to guarantee its particular role as intervention or event at work in political movements, since speech that constitutes the sexual self rather than expressing it could still (and does so for Foucault) easily remain in the service of hegemonic techniques of management. To put it simply, showing that sexual practices are effects of discourse rather than the other way around by itself does nothing to account for something like "speaking the sexual" as resistance, where resistance truly exceeds hegemonic norms and offers something like intervention and insurgency. Accounting for the latter requires a model of the relations between sex, language, and power that shows how speaking the sexual can create conditions of freedom, rather than showing how it grants access to social power. It requires a return to the idea of language, rather than bodies, as the site of the event.

Jean-François Lyotard offers a way of thinking intervention or insurgency in language when he distinguishes between its figural function and its discursive function. The figural happens when language has an effect in the world that cannot be exhausted by what happens on the discursive level. A poem, for instance, "does something" that cannot be exhaustively explained by looking at the contents of the poem's language. That "something" is what Lyotard calls "figure," and it is what puts us in touch with the unrepresentable, even as we speak, write, represent. Speech necessarily always exceeds what is said.

In Lyotard's texts, speech is from its beginnings interlocution, taking place among multiple subjects entering into a social relation. Speech and the state are coconstitutive. He argues that interlocution is the necessary condition for the state because from the fact of interlocution arises "an *effect of right*. If any human being *can* be an interlocutor for other human beings, he must *be able to*, that is, must be enabled or allowed to" (1993, 140). The social is a field of interlocutors, and speech takes place in a sphere that is social from the start. Thus, to silence someone in an interlocutory relationship is to attack their belonging to civil society. The problem lies in silencing not the contents of their speech but the fact of speech, the "speaking" itself. Likewise, merely clearing the way for them to speak is not enough to guarantee the metaright: freedom of speech here means not getting out of the way of a preexisting, fully formed interiority seeking externalization, but creating the conditions for the interiority itself.

How does this happen? A certain outside-ness, or estrangement from oneself, is the essential first moment in the formation of the social. Estrangement is the moment in which I am taken hostage by the Other-in-me and forced into a passive silence so that I may hear what it is I will say. The figural function of language has precisely this effect: as an event, as something that simply happens (rather than being deployed by a subject), it is the moment of discursive passivity, a stupor that makes listening possible. Only following this silence or stupor am I able to say something, "something other than the *déja dit* (what has already been said)," rather than repeating and conserving existing meanings (1993, 143). Thus, figure is the condition of the possibility of interlocution, "the Other that language is" (145). For Lyotard, the condition of the possibility of civil society is simultaneously the condition of the possibility of saying something new. Unlike the sedimented clichés of rhetoric, which conserve the status quo, the "new" is that after which nothing will ever be the same again. This "something new" speaks through me only insofar as I am estranged from myself. I am not properly "my" self and don't know yet what it is I will say. Lyotard connects the notion of a self detached from itself with a speech that is productive/constitutive and "new" rather than a conduit for preexisting, sedimented truisms.

Baudrillard makes a similar point is his writing against a certain epistemic authority of first-person accounts:

> You have to be a stranger to something to speak about it in a strange—that is to say original—way. You have to be a man to speak of the feminine. All those who speak from "experience" speak in a conventional way—they relate their life stories. In fact, you have absolutely to collude in what you are speaking about and at the same time to be somewhere else altogether. You have to love it and hate it. You have to be the thing you speak of and to be violently against it. This is the law of hospitality, and it is the law of hostility. ([1997] 2007, 46–47)

It may be more true to say "you have to be a feminist to speak of the feminine," since no one better fulfills the requirement of being the thing she speaks of and being violently against it. The focus is on a dehiscence, on being "beside oneself" (to quote Judith Butler's title) in order for something unexpected or "evental" to happen. With this more nuanced notion of speech, in which the confessing subject becomes the subject of not just interpretation but transformation (rather than a subject liberated from repression), the idea of "giving voice" to prostitute discourses or the speech of pornographic women takes on special value, even for feminism. On this model, rather than speech simply representing what is, the very fact of speaking itself makes possible intervention and transformation—of the sex industry, of sexualities, of gender relations.

Thus, the charge made by cyberlibertarians that antipornography feminism shuts down the speech of women and sexual minorities becomes quite serious in ways that the antiporn position should take seriously. The risk is that of shutting down not the speech that we don't want to hear, or what, for example, some academic feminists imagine some sex workers might say, but the speech central to all feminist and all liberationist interests, because it means the very possibility of social change. At stake is the very future of the political speech that we have, precisely, not yet heard. We thus confront two (related) arguments for why pornography may be important for freedom: the Foucauldian argument for the production of pleasure and bodily limit experiences, and the Lyotardian argument for the transformative political power of the very fact of speaking. What remains to be examined is whether the social effects of "speaking the sexual" enable or constrain social change. Internet pornography changes the stakes of this examination by forcing the related question, *What kinds of speech are enabled and/or constrained by Internet technologies?*

THE INTERNET AND THE EVENT

In the introduction to the second edition of *Defending Pornography: Free Speech, Sex, and the Fight for Women's Rights* (2000), Strossen writes that Internet pornography provokes unprecedented anxieties about "sexual expression" (she prefers this phrase to "pornography") and a renewal of tendencies toward censorship. For Wendy Kaminer, author of the foreword, this has to do with generational differences: parents, with their natural tendencies to control their children's behavior, feel suddenly less in control because their children are more comfortable with computer technology than they themselves are (ix). Thus, in Kaminer's account, the motivation to censorship is purely psychological and subjective, emotional (fear, need to control), rather than ideological, political, or inspired by some moral code extending beyond the individual: "the more people feel controlled by culture (and the less they feel in sync with it), the more their drive to censor" (ix). For Strossen herself, the Internet introduces nothing new to the political struggles over pornography. It pits two timeworn American ideological traditions against each other: the cybercensors, inheritors of American Puritanism, and the cyberlibertarians, inheritors of the First Amendment—two positions as old as the proverbial hills (xiv–xv). Both Kaminer's foreword and Strossen's new introduction were added to the new edition of *Defending Pornography* in order to show the book's relevance for Internet pornography, but in neither is there the slightest hint that Internet technologies are in fact deeply "new," in the sense of profoundly transforming the experience of pornography, or that such a transformation of the experience might have important effects beyond that experience. Strossen's position is that the field of sexual expression or communication is continuous and homogeneous, with the new technology of the Internet merely extending it further, faster. "*Defending Pornography*'s bottom line conclusion—that defending freedom of expression is essential for advocates of women's rights, as well as equality rights more broadly—remains as true in cyberspace as it has been in other contexts" (xix).

Though she is no cyberlibertarian, Williams, like Strossen, sees pornography as being on the side of transgression rather than patriarchal hegemony, loosely speaking. In significant contrast to Strossen, however, she focuses on the discontinuities that the new forms of pornography present. As we have seen, for Williams the proliferation of amateur and queer or "other," nonnormative pornography that the Internet makes possible completely changes the terms of the debate. In other words, the Internet introduces such fundamental changes to the distribution and consumption of pornography that pornographic discourse itself changes, in terms of the contents of the imagery and of its social role. Thus, it would be "in the profusion rather than the censoring of pornographies" that feminists could find the potential for resistance of dominant heteronormative discourses of pleasure (Williams 1992, 262).

Williams's work introduces the very important and I think correct impression that the political belonging of pornography changes over time. She uses the plural form "pornographies" to underscore that there are many different sexual tastes which the market reflects and that the tastes and the pornography are both historical phenomena, to be treated as such. I would like to add to this that the relationship between pornography and the rest of culture, law, and politics is also historical, which means that any answer to the question, *Is pornography hegemonic (part of the problem) or transgressive (part of the solution)?* depends on the state of that relationship at a particular time. The question cannot be answered abstractly.

While Williams argues that the Internet increases pornography's potential to be transgressive rather than normative, however, I contend that Internet pornography, with its unique logic of distribution and consumption, compromises the progressive potential of pornographic speech for reasons that have to do with the broader social meaning of the medium. This is what interests me and what I believe should interest contemporary feminist engagements with this issue: What happens to pornographic speech when it is subjected to the particular logic of distribution and consumption the Internet provides? How does becoming an Internet phenomenon affect pornography's function as a normalizing discourse? Alternatively, how does it affect possibilities for pornography to be—or become—transgressive and interventionist?

The qualitatively different nature of Internet pornography forces us to revisit the problem of speech precisely because the technology raises new anxieties about the social function of signs, about speech and its material effects. If Foucault would argue that we cannot talk about pornography without considering the interlacings of sex, discourse, and power, then Internet pornography brings this necessity to a new level of urgency. Cyberporn's impressive growth rate is a constant reminder that ours is a social order more tuned into (and turned on by) signs, representations, simulacra—and their limitless circulation—than ever before in history. From this it follows not that the practice paradigm should be abandoned but that it is not sufficient in mapping the social effects of pornography in the Internet age. After all, the use of computers is itself a material practice that resonates along axes of race, gender, class, location, and so on. This inquiry, however, concerns the experience of pornography not as viewed on computer screens but specifically as experienced as part of a "world wide web." Internet pornography demands the reconception of pornography once again, this time as neither ideas (as in the traditional speech paradigm) nor materials (as in the practice paradigm), but information, and as subject to the logic of the democratization of information as well as to new fantasies of immateriality. The fact that it is presently possible to view pornography on cell phones and not just laptops troubles the relationship between materiality and semiosis in this sexual practice in unprecedented ways. Pornography conceived as information requires what N. Katherine Hayles calls a suppression and forgetting of materiality and of information's fundamental dependency on a medium (1999, 13).[3] Thus, my claim that cyberporn is best conceived of as speech if we wish to examine its social effects, and in particular question pornography's relationship to freedom, is not essentialist, or a wholesale embracing of this forgetting, but rather the opposite: contingent, instrumental, a "definition" in direct response to a historical situation.

It may be possible to reconfigure the cyberlibertarian position in these terms: legal restrictions on pornographic materials run the risk of simultaneously compromising real, evental speech, the kind that feminism and all liberationist projects need, be it understood in terms of speech acts or the figural function of language. This position works on the assumption of a separation between pornographic and evental speech, arguing that if you want the latter, you simply have to put up with a bit of the former. A very different position argues that pornographic speech itself provides particular conditions for events, figures, or acts to occur. Williams and Kipnis theorize *the value of pornography itself* for feminist interests, emphasizing fantasy, perversity, displacement, complexity, and women's sexual pleasure. This kind of defense interests me the most because it is here that Internet distribution poses the most serious obstacles.

Gilbert offers a compelling response to the feminist drive to censor pornography on the grounds that it eroticizes violence, especially sexual violence against women. It is the revolutionary consciousness itself, she writes, which eroticizes violence and is fascinated by the idea of irrational, uncontrollable sexualities. In other words, it is not by accident that Sade emerges directly from the violence of the French Revolution.

> Certainly, fictions in which "love and death" have a dialogue—or, to be more exact, in which they howl their confusion of identity—appear to have burst from the French Revolution and Sade like a need, not a fashion. . . . If we consider that women's revolution against the power of the father, the family, the whole "patriarchal state" both echoes and multiplies the exhilaration and terror of 1789, then is it not possible that women's need for a literature in which sex and violence, love and death, can wrestle with one another is as great as—perhaps even greater than—men's? (1992, 228–29)

Gilbert's point here is not that we should not censor violent pornography because it's pleasurable, but because it may be read as a productive "quarrel with Enlightenment trust in reason, science, and people's potential once freed from religious superstition . . . , an illustration of the wrongness of those who insist that nature, human or otherwise, would, if left to its own devices, be 'virtuous'" (225). She shows that it is possible to read Andrea Dworkin's quasi-autobiographical fiction *Mercy* as pornography, following in the tradition of Sade's *Justine*. "It could well be argued that Dworkin's novel is more—or at least as—likely as Sade's to persuade the reader that violence, power, and pain are the whole of sexuality (and not just male sexuality; we are offered no female alternative) and even to create the feeling that this is in some way horribly exciting" (222). The claim is supposed to provoke, since Dworkin's novel is presented as a work of man-hating, "radical" feminism in which heterosexual relations are irreducibly violent and thus condemnable, while in Sade violence and women's insatiable masochism are famously, orgiastically celebrated. This disjunction between what is ostensibly intended and how a work may be received is precisely at the heart of Gilbert's argument against censorship. No one can know whether or not what she or he writes will be arousing (and to whom), and thus used as pornography.

> The truth is that this "pornography," for which so many people are hunting, lives not in the product but beyond it, in the active relationship between product and reader. Pedophiles sometimes masturbate while looking through catalogues of children's clothes, or watching choirboys singing in "Songs of Praise." . . . Because we have laughably little idea about what anyone, male or female, is actually doing when writing or reading about sexuality and violence, we are in no position, either moral or practical, even to attempt to stop them. (223–24, 229)

Gilbert is correct that texts circulate in the world in ways that cannot be controlled, and pornographic texts are no different in this respect. This is at the heart of Jennifer Saul's argument that works of pornography do not constitute speech acts: "A work of pornography is not an utterance in a context. The reason for this is simple. A work of pornography, such as a film, can be used in many different contexts. . . . Only utterances in contexts can be speech acts, so works of pornography cannot be speech acts" (2006, 234). And yet clearly, when we take into account not only that Internet pornography is structurally circulatable, like every other text, but that it is *in fact* actively, excessively circulated, the question of how pornography acts on the world cannot be easily dismissed on the grounds that it does not fulfill speech act theory's criteria.

There is an important distinction to be made between Sade and Dworkin on one hand, and the children's clothing catalogs and choirboy scenes on the other. *Mercy* echoes *Justine* precisely because both are not (or not merely) pornography but literature, or because both works have a wide open "beyond" to them into which so many different things may be projected. This revolutionary energy, if I may call it that, of the dialogue between sex and violence is what makes it impossible to describe real literature as "normative." Sade's pornographic scenes of mother-daughter incest, coupled with feces-eating, group urination, and all the women ejaculating all over each other—all scenes from another novel, *Juliette*—for instance, cannot be read as "normative" in any sense. Likewise, the scenes of rape in *Mercy* are also scenes of madness, of the breakdown of intelligibility and norms and language. These are claims one would have a hard time making of the children's clothes catalogs and choirboy scenes that might arouse the pedophile. For the same reason it is difficult to image them in the role of texts from which the call to revolution emerges, as it does from both Dworkin and Sade.

Gilbert could perhaps have made her point even more strongly had she moved from literature which may be read as pornographic to materials which are intended as pornographic at the time of production but function nonpornographically in new contexts of citation. *Semiotext(e) USA* (Lotringer 1987) offers a great example of this. Pages 106–9 of the anthology are left blank with only large, diagonal letters reading "CENSORED (See Enclosures)." The "enclosures" are folded and sealed in a plastic pouch glued to the book's back cover, with stamped text that reads: "Calling it 'subversive' and 'obscene,' five book printers in the spring of 1987 refused to print *Semiotext(e) USA*. A sixth printer agreed to do all but four pages, which we have printed separately and include here." The pages make up a sort of montage of pornographic photos and literary text, including a quote about male sexual aggression by Dworkin from *Pornography: Men Possessing Women*. This almost theatrical performance of the distinctly American struggle over pornography, literature, freedom of speech, violence, censorship, gender, and transgression is located at the center (in the blank pages) and periphery of this book simultaneously. The photographs do not function pornographically here, and they certainly do not function normatively in any straightforward sense.

However, if pornography may be read as normative at all—and clearly this kind of reading is at the heart of so many critiques of pornography, both feminist and conservative—it is precisely because it is not sufficiently mad. Whatever is normative is somehow, even in its most violent incarnations, acceptable in, adaptable to, functioning descriptively and/or didactically in the world. Accepting this critique, however, does not commit one to the idea that the way in which pornography affects norms remains stable over time. On the contrary, my argument depends on the possibility that pornography's role in the production of norms changes throughout history and in response to the changes in the relations between sex, speech, and power. We know from historians that the contents of pornography change over time (in British pornography from the eighteenth century, for instance, the reigning themes were flagellation of men by governesses, catholic themes, and domestic scenes, in contrast to themes central to contemporary pornography; see Peakman 2003), but it is also possible that the very role of pornography in the production of norms changes as well.

This is precisely the argument that Baudrillard makes, proposing that new relationships between discourse and power in the age of information, in which Internet pornography plays a significant role, affect the ability of the body politic to produce something like "meaning" at all. If he is right, this has consequences for both the cyberlibertarian and the (let's call it) "revolutionary fantasist" position that porn should exist unregulated by the state precisely because of its role in the production of resistant discourses. Is it possible for pornography to be evental? If Gilbert is right about *Justine* and *Mercy*, the answer is clearly yes. But is this because of *some* pornography's capacity to act as literature in some circumstances and as art in others? If so, is it also possible that Internet pornography does not meet the necessary criteria to become evental, and instead cuts itself off from the possibility of acting as literature, art, or madness? Indeed, as the following chapter shows, according to Baudrillard, today's Internet pornography is complicit in, even central to, the production of a body politic which can neither speak nor listen in interventionist ways.

3 DEMOCRACY AND THE

INFORMATION SOCIETY

THE OBSCENE AND THE PRIVATE

More than a decade before the appearance of the World Wide Web, in a short essay called "The Ecstasy of Communication," Baudrillard describes what he calls "the categorical imperative of communication," an incessant pressure to make visible and exteriorize everything hidden and interior ([1983] 1991, 132). Prior to the advent of today's information society, he writes, the society of the spectacle functioned according to alienation and representation. "It is not obscenity—the spectacle is never obscene" because it is perpetually "on scene," at a distance. But communication collapses distance and reduces alienation to immediacy. Spectacle vanishes.

> Obscenity begins precisely when there is no more spectacle, no more scene, when all becomes transparence and immediate visibility, when everything is exposed to the harsh and inexorable light of information and communication. . . . It is no longer then the traditional obscenity of what is hidden, repressed, forbidden, or obscure; on the contrary, it is the obscenity of the visible, of the all-too-visible, of the more-visible-than-visible. It is the obscenity of what no longer has any secret, of what dissolves completely in information and communication. (130–31)

The information society is like America distilled to its purest form, namely the road trip "out West," in terms of both social imaginary and visceral subjective experience. It is an experience of "the America of the vain and absolute liberty of freeways . . . , the one of desert-like speed, of motels and mineral surfaces," distillable to the desert, which is "no more than that: an ecstatic critique of culture, and ecstatic form of disappearance" (1987, 48). Sexuality and the body undergo what he calls "desertification," taking on a transparency and lightness, losing their materiality and opacity. Amnesia, asceticism, surface, desert, heat, dazzle, the fractal geometry of minerals in geological formations: these are the images Baudrillard invokes in his account of the ultimate road trip, the one which leaves behind the trappings of the Old World, of memory, history, fatigue, alienation, and with them, spectacle and representation. America is neither dream nor reality, but "hyperreality," where simulation becomes reality itself. "Americans, for their part, have no sense of simulation. . . . they are themselves simulation in its most developed state" ([1986] 1999, 28–29).

We should thus not be surprised by the recent large-scale obsession with self-expression on American television: reality TV, talk shows on which people air their most private problems ("Dr. Phil," for instance), politicians and other celebrities holding press conferences in which they apologize for their sexual misadventures, and so on. Whether or not reality TV actually "is" real is a secondary question from this perspective. What matters is the need for the experience of the real, however mediated and simulated it is in fact, and its direct link to a fantasy of community. Kipnis points to the obsession with reality TV as an issue of class difference:

> What's often referred to as the tabloidization of American culture also reflects shifting standards of public and private. When lower-middle America takes to the airwaves to brandish the intimate details of their lives—their secret affairs, their marital skirmishes, their familial contretemps—and talk show guests duke it out on air, high-minded critics

> invariably respond with contemptuous little think pieces snorting
> about what bad taste all this is. (1999, 172–73)

What we call "taste," she points out, has always been a concept shot
through with assumptions about class, which lie at the roots of our
critiques of these tendencies toward self-exposure. But television is
no longer the privileged medium for putting oneself on public display. The Internet has made showing oneself the favorite activity of
American upper-middle-class twenty- and thirty-somethings, on
Facebook, Twitter, Tumblr, and endless blogs, such as Emma Koenig's recent "Fuck! I'm in My Twenties," a blog about the mundane
details of Koenig's mundane, admittedly privileged, young life.
Despite the lack of any interesting content, Koenig's blog has been
turned into a book, is becoming a TV show, and has been written
about in the *New York Times*, as cited in The Atlantic Wire.[1]

Baudrillard might argue that the popularity of Koenig's blog is
not in spite of its lack of content but because of it. "This is a society that is endlessly concerned to vindicate itself, seeking to justify
its own existence. Everything has to be made public: what you are
worth, what you earn, how you live. . . . The society's look is a self-
publicizing one" ([1986] 1999, 85–86). For him, as well as for
Lyotard, self-exposure is a matter not of taste but of large-scale
shifts in the body politic, its self-definition and conceptions of its
own governability. Baudrillard's reading of the obscenity of communication aligns perfectly with Lyotard's critique of the modern
democratic state, of which the United States is the prime example.
They are connected by a logic of democratization.

In conditions of totalitarianism, the state begins from the
assumption that its subjects are, precisely, alienated. They do not
surrender unconditionally. Since they harbor secrets, force may be
used, secret police may be dispatched, phones may be bugged,
citizens may be imprisoned and interrogated, and so on. The democratic state, in contrast, wants not to use any of these coercions
and thus requires a political subject that is completely unalien-
ated, transparent, and committed, with nothing hidden, nothing

held back. Communication becomes an internal imperative rather than something forcibly imposed from the outside.

In his book *Privacy: A Manifesto*, sociologist Wolfgang Sofsky traces the disappearance of privacy to the French Revolution, which "launched an attack on private life unprecedented in the Western world" in the name of democratic ideals universally shared (2008, 27). Accordingly, the most democratic state translates power into the becoming transparent of subjects with the help of surveillance technologies. "It wants to know everything, all the time, everywhere" (20–21). Lyotard's critique of democracy ([1993] 1997b) is at the same time a critique of communicability and transparency. Lyotard holds that in every individual subject of rights there is a "secret," a part of existence that is absolutely not subject to anything. It is not our humanity but the condition of the very humanity that can claim that rights are owed to it. "Rights and respect for rights are owed to us only because something in us exceeds every recognized right" (121). Following the writer Nina Berberova, he contrasts the "secret life" with the "general life," which is another name for how contemporary democracy, rooted in liberal humanism, understands the political subject to whom basic rights are owed. The "general life" position begins from the assumption that a whole, self-contained, self-identical individual preexists democratic relations, into which she enters by means of clear, transparent communication. Conditioned by this imaginary, modern democracy is "haunted by the suspicion that there is something that escapes [it], that might plot against [it]. [Democracy] needs the whole soul, and . . . need[s] it to surrender unconditionally" (118).

Blogging is the best contemporary manifestation of the general life. In "Why I Blog," Andrew Sullivan (2008) writes that

> the historic form closest to blogs is the diary. But with this difference: a diary is almost always a private matter. Its raw honesty, its dedication to marking life as it happens and remembering life as it was, makes it a terrestrial log. A few diaries are meant to be read by others, of course,

just as correspondence could be—but usually posthumously, or as a way to compile facts for a more considered autobiographical rendering. But a blog, unlike a diary, is instantly public. It transforms this most personal and retrospective of forms into a painfully public and immediate one. It combines the confessional genre with the log form and exposes the author in a manner no author has ever been exposed before.

The democratic state denies the subject her secret existence, Lyotard continues, by pressuring her to exert her rights at all times, to be exhaustively, absolutely public. One must be crazy not to exercise rights one has! "Why didn't you say this, do that? You had the right!" (120). Indeed, Sullivan writes, he knew that as a freelance writer he "needed to have a presence online" long before he knew what to blog about. "I had no clear idea of what to do, but a friend who ran a Web-design company offered to create a site for me," creating a blank space in response to the pressure to simply exist online—all of it prior to the formation of any ideas about what, exactly, to write (Sullivan 2008). Clearly, this pressure to exercise one's rights at all times is in direct conflict with secrecy. "If you are not public, you disappear; if not exposed as much as possible, you don't exist. Your no-man's-land is interesting only if expressed and communicated. Heavy pressures are put on silence, to give birth to expression" (Lyotard [1993] 1997b, 120). The categorical imperative of communication fits perfectly within the modern democratic framework, where all secrets are supposed to be exposed in order to ensure the transparency of the governable subject.

PORNOGRAPHY AND THE REAL

Pornography appears as a trope in numerous literary critiques of totalitarianism. For instance, Peter Esterhazy writes about the pornographic conditions of dictatorship in his book *A Little Hungarian Pornography*. "Life in a dictatorship is different than life in a democracy. You live in a different way. And you write in a different way. You also read in a different way." He presents the pornographic as the order of lies and invites the reader to "imagine, if we can, a country where everything is a lie" (quoted in Cornell 2000, 606). "Such a total, all encompassing lie, when from history through green-pea soup, when from our father's eyebrows and our lover's lap everything is a lie, not to mention this theoretical yet very tangible presence of threat, all this makes for a highly poetic situation" (607). There are only lies and secrets, fictions and delusions, including the illusion of democracy itself. Polish writer Witold Gombrowicz's 1960 novel, *Pornografia*, set in the rural outskirts of Nazi-occupied Poland, is about two men becoming obsessed with forcing two local adolescents into a seemingly undesired romantic relationship. The narrative itself has nothing overtly to do with pornography but revolves around the presentation of a virtual, staged experience being presented as natural and spontaneous.[2] These uses of the concept of pornography as related to artifice and force underscore the contrast Lyotard explores, in which true democracy means transparency, the absence of lies or secrets, an absence that presumably renders the democratic situation unpoetic, but also unpornographic.

In contrast to Esterhazy and Gombrowicz, Baudrillard makes pornography a matter of truth and democracy, not lies and totalitarianism. He continues his exploration of obscenity and communication in *Seduction*, turning to pornography in particular. The proliferation of pornographies made possible by Internet technologies makes the word "obscene" more than just a dramatic choice of adjective in the case of this particular aspect of the information society. Pornography is communication, in the sense of the disappearance of spectacle and the imperative to complete transparence. According to an ancient metaphysics that his book reanimates, truth, or sex, is of the order of the masculine, while artifice, veiling, and seduction are of the order of the feminine. That this way of figuring the feminine is problematic from feminist perspectives is obvious. For instance, I support Sara Ahmed's conclusion that in his analysis of the transvestite subject "what

Baudrillard is celebrating is precisely women's status as signs and commodities circulated by and for male spectators and consumers" (1996, 82). But this tension between Baudrillard's apparently antifeminist celebration of a problematically figured femininity and the feminist struggle to rearticulate the feminine in more mobile, irreverent, and fluid ways is precisely the point in his work. The criticism that he has merely echoed an old, essentialist binary has been wielded against Luce Irigaray and other thinkers who rely on an essentialism they call "strategic" or "mimetic."[3]

Baudrillard makes the case that all pornography, no matter how hard or soft, is the ultimate medium of masculinity, but not because it has anything to do with power, or with men's power over women's bodies. Instead, pornography is hypermasculine because it makes sex hyperreal, more detailed and better than the real thing. Like America, pornography is hyperreality, pure simulation, endless circulation of commodities. "Pornography is the quadrophonics of sex. It adds a third and fourth track to the sexual act. It is the hallucination of detail that rules. . . . End of the secret. What else does pornography do, in its sham vision, than reveal the inexorable, microscopic truth of sex?" ([1979] 1990, 31). Thus, Baudrillard argues, pornography and the feminine are like oil and water—and in our pornographic culture the seductive power of the feminine is disappearing rapidly, leaving behind only this babbling quadrophonics of sex. He condemns this erasure of the feminine, but not because it causes harm to women in particular. Everyone suffers from the disappearance of the feminine. Pornography is not just one genre among others in the information society. As the genre whose task it is to expose precisely the most secret thing, pornography is the ultimate manifestation of the ecstasy of communication.

Ursula K. LeGuin's essay "Why Are Americans Afraid of Dragons?" argues that the American lack of tolerance for science fiction and fantasy is symptomatic of a macho, puritanical, sexually repressed, and politically inert society.

> Nowadays with our secular Puritanism, the man who refuses to read
> novels because it's unmanly to do so, or because they aren't true, will
> most likely end up watching bloody detective thrillers on the televi-
> sion, or reading hack Westerns or sports stories, or going in for por-
> nography, from *Playboy* on down. It is his starved imagination, craving
> nourishment, that forces him to do so. But he can rationalize such
> entertainment by saying that it is realistic—after all, sex exists, and
> there are criminals, and there are baseball players, and there used to be
> cowboys—and also by saying that it is virile, by which he means that
> it doesn't interest most women. (37)

Since every subject's imagination needs cultivation, the subject
that fears fantasy must turn somewhere for that cultivation, somewhere it imagines to be safely "real" and free of fantasy. It turns to
pornography precisely because porn allows us to imagine that it
shows the real. For LeGuin, then, we unfortunately look at pornography instead of reading a great novel. For Baudrillard, in contrast, the interest in the real has nothing to do with postpuritanical
"repression." American political subjectivity in particular cannot
tolerate secrecy and occlusion. It is not that Americans cannot
stand what pornography makes visible because they are so
repressed or repressive, but the opposite: they are so *ex*pressive
that nothing remains hidden, and the hidden is what they fear
most—the dragon in its lair, never seen in daytime, announcing
itself only obliquely, by means of terrifying sounds escaping some
subterranean darkness. It is seduction, not pornography, that
Americans cannot stand.

A related but slightly different way to think about the question
of the real is with the help of Foucault's critique of the repressive
hypothesis ([1978] 1990). The dominant idea, Foucault writes, is
that sex is repressed and must be freed by "the removing of an
obstacle, the breaking of a secret." But all this hypothesis does is
generate so much discourse on the subject that what takes place in
fact is the proliferation of discourses about sex, rather than their

repression. "Is it not with the aim of inciting people to speak of sex that it is made to mirror, at the outer limit of every actual discourse, something akin to a secret whose discovery is imperative, a thing abusively reduced to silence . . . ?" (34–35). The very question whether or not pornography shows/says something *real* about sex is intelligible only in the context of the repressive hypothesis, against the backdrop of the basic assumption that *there is a truth of sex*, that this truth/reality of sex is repressed, and finally that it must be liberated by expression. In fact, Foucault argues, the juxtaposition between secrecy/silence/repression on one hand and discourse/truth/knowledge on the other, is a false dichotomy in the case of the discursive production of sexuality. More importantly, it is not only false but essential to this discursive production: the obsessive maintenance of the tension between them is at the heart of the modern idea of sexuality, ensuring its status as never merely a banal, empirical fact but always as a problem to be managed by means of ever new techniques.

Thus, for Foucault, sex is not just one idea among others in modernity. Sex troubles the real, and our capacity to see it, say it, and come to know it, in uniquely powerful ways. The imperative to confess the sexual, which over time transforms sex into an object of knowledge and a problem of truth, functions at the same time to maintain secrecy around sex. Sex must be confessed because it is secret and "one confesses one's crimes, one's sins, one's thoughts and desires, one's illnesses and troubles; one goes about telling, with the greatest precision, whatever is most difficult to tell" (59). By means of this elaborate apparatus, the illusion is created that secrets are being divulged in the service of arriving at the truth about oneself and one's inner life. The dimensions of secrecy and truth are both simply effects of the *scientia sexualis* that marks Western modernity. They are simply two sides of the same coin.

For Lyotard and Baudrillard, secrecy is radically heterogeneous to the dimension of truth and the creation of sex as an object of knowledge. It is what escapes democracy in fact, not merely in the social imaginary. It is the reason that the imperative must be reiterated as an imperative rather than just becoming what citizens naturally do. Democracy calls for communication because there is in fact something that escapes it. On this model, it is illegitimate to call the secret "sex," as Foucault does, because it is so outside the system that we simply do not know what it is.

SHOWING "IT"

Kipnis suggests that it is crucial to read pornographic materials not as real but as a form of science fiction or other speculative fiction which "imagines different futures": "One model for looking at pornography would be as a kind of science fiction; that is, as a fantasy about futurity, whose setting is the present. We don't get offended when science fiction imagines different futures, even dystopic ones set in worlds that look like our own" (200). Indeed, there is clearly something complex taking place in the way that pornography manipulates our experience of what is real, like other genres of visual and narrative fiction. However, the comparison with science fiction might benefit from some more nuanced distinctions among types of SF, such as what Baudrillard offers: "Two kinds of science fiction. The one fantastical and fabulous, playing on other worlds; the other paroxystic, extrapolating a detail, a characteristic feature and, by a rigorous logic, revealing its eccentricity or its extreme effects" ([1997] 2007, 117). Kipnis clearly makes her analogy with the first kind in mind: "What would the world look like if men were emotionally and romantically compatible with women? . . . So pornography's fantasy is also one of gender malleability" (200). But perhaps it is the second model, the paroxystic, that is more suitable for comparison with pornography. One of Baudrillard's privileged examples of this kind of SF is the work of J. G. Ballard.

Indeed, in Ballard's novel *Cocaine Nights*, a murder mystery set in a society in which resources and leisure time are unlimited, the extrapolated detail which reveals the entire social logic is related to the problematics of pornography. Though it is set on the Costa del Sol in Spain, the place Ballard describes distinctly echoes Baudrillard's descriptions of the "American" West: "Perhaps this was what a leisure-dominated future would resemble? Nothing could ever happen in this affectless realm, where entropic drift calmed the surfaces of a thousand swimming pools" (1996, 35). The novel makes this point repeatedly: it's not that nothing *bad* could happen in a place this idyllic, but that nothing *at all* could happen in a place this devoid of affect.

> The retirement pueblos lay by the motorway, embalmed in a dream of the sun from which they would never awake. As always, when I drove along the coast to Marbella, I seemed to be moving through a zone accessible only to a neuroscientist, and scarcely at all to a travel writer. The white facades of the villas and apartment houses were like blocks of time that had crystallized beside the road. Here on the Costa del Sol nothing would ever happen again. (75)

But of course the novel is about precisely this—something happening in a place where nothing could happen. *Cocaine Nights* is a novel about the event taking place in a Baudrillardian future-present.

Ballard's novels are famously sexual, but sex plays a unique role in this story by underlining the society's lack of affect in response to rape. As the protagonist learns more and more about the community, he realizes that real rape has taken on the status of a strange game involving group voyeurism. The first rape scene takes place in the public car park at night. Upon breaking up the assault, while the bruised woman collects her torn clothes and retches on the gravel, the protagonist makes a surprising discovery: a row of cars in which passengers clad in evening wear had been watching the rape without intervening, "like a gallery audience at an exclusive private view" (58). For Ballard, the moral and emotional response to rape as something to be consumed voyeuristically is not just an accidental feature of this particular place but is in fact characteristic of this kind of society. In the event that this could still be read as spectacle rather than simulacrum, however, Ballard ventures further into the collapsing of the real into the hyperreal. One chapter of the book is devoted to a description of a porno-graphic film in which there is a staged lesbian and straight scene, after which two men enter the room and really rape the fictional "bride." The women are clearly amateurs, and only the "brides-maids" know what's about to happen.

> The lens steadied itself, and caught the bodies of two naked men who had broken into the bedroom from the balcony and hurled themselves across the floor. The bridesmaids seized their waists and pulled them onto the bed. The bride alone seemed startled, trying to hide her naked body behind the wedding dress . . . I watched the rape run its course, trying to avoid the desperate eyes crushed into the satin bed-spread. The bride was no longer acting or colluding with the camera. The lesbian porno-film had been a set-up, designed to lure her to this anonymous apartment, the mise-en-scene for a real rape for which the bridesmaids, but not the heroine, had been prepared. (126)

The film shows sex taking place under multiple circumstances simultaneously—staged, acted sex filmed simultaneously with the real rape—both of them real in completely different ways, and at the same time not quite real because they are filmed. The scene ends with the porn "actress" smiling at the camera. Still an ama-teur, she had finally figured out this was part of the plan, part of the work of acting in pornography. She had fulfilled the task cor-rectly: "Yet she managed to smile at the camera, the plucky starlet facing the massed lenses of Fleet Street, or a brave child swallow-ing an unpleasant medicine for her own good" (127). Ballard's protagonist finds none of this any more arousing than the rest. The chapter "The Pornographic Film" ends with the smiling "bride," a meditation on the real in pornography, where the layers of simulation upon simulation have created precisely a state of the hyperreal, problematizing the possibility of witnessing, documentation, and evidence in this murder mystery.

Erotica writer and former sex worker Scarlet the Harlot writes in her online journal (2010), "I'll willingly give said blow job in exchange for dinner, not because I'm particularly hungry, but because there's something deliciously courtesanesque about it, and let's face it, it'll be great blog fodder." In some older feminist anti-pornography materials, a striking image was often deployed, namely that of a woman literally silenced by a penis in her mouth. For instance, Carole Pateman asks in *The Sexual Contract*, "Could it be conjectured that men's current widespread demand to buy women's bodies to penetrate their mouths is connected to the revitalization of the feminist movement and women's demand to speak?" (1988, 259, n33). Baudrillard reminds us that the quadrophonic screams of today's "ecstatic" woman on the computer screen, ever more "ecstatic" in ever more interesting and different positions and erotic situations, *say* nothing. The more Scarlet blogs, the less she actually says. These "expressions" tell us nothing "new" but instead serve the important function of reinforcing the categorical imperative of communication, as we see in Scarlet's completely *uncritical* ("let's face it") valuing of a sexual encounter as "blog fodder." We have witnessed a shift in the logic of consumption of bought sex, from the modern urban prostitute as "spectacle," as grotesque and carnivalesque female body (see Bell 1994, 141), to pornography as immediacy and transparency, the vanishing of both alienation and desire in a frenzy of the visible, of signifiers circulating without any anchoring in referents.

Linda Williams argues against the idea that this shift is all that complete. While the goal of pornography is indeed to show "it," this goal is often not satisfied, and this failure is central to the pornographic imaginary. The tension between seeing and not seeing "the truth of pleasure," what she calls the "crisis of the visibility of pleasure," marks the pornographic text. Her analysis focuses on "sexual fantasy, role play, and performance, none of which is a

self-evidently visible, unfakeable truth, nor necessarily genital"
(1992, 241). While Williams points to porn's failure to meet its
alleged goal of showing "it," Baudrillard's concern is less with the
fact of what is shown and more with the goal itself. His description of pornography as "the quadrophonics of sex" is not about
what is actually visible but about the endless circulation of signs
and collapse of simulation into reality. As the following chapter
shows, Internet porn in particular thematizes this goal as it unfolds
according to the logic of the limitless circulation of information.
Internet porn exhibits the imperative of communication in unique
and powerful ways, conflating sex and hyperreality and irrevocably linking pornography to the problematics of democracy and
political ontology in general. The following passage in which
Foucault traces the shifts in sexual discourses in the Victorian
period describes something akin to the qualitative changes to pornography that have taken place since the advent of Internet
distribution.

> There was a steady proliferation of discourses concerned with sex—
> specific discourses, different from one another both by their form and
> by their object: a discursive ferment that gathered momentum from
> the eighteenth century onward. Here I am thinking not so much of
> the probable increase in "illicit" discourses, that is, discourses of infrac-
> tion that crudely named sex by way of insult or mockery of the new
> code of decency; the tightening up of the rules of decorum likely did
> produce, as a countereffect, a valorization and intensification of inde-
> cent speech. But more important was the multiplication of discourses
> concerning sex in the field of the exercise of power itself: an institu-
> tional incitement to speak about it and to do so more and more.
> ([1978] 1990, 18)

In the case of the Internet, *the field of the exercise of power becomes
coextensive with the field of the exercise of speech*; a proliferation of
discourses imagine themselves to be spontaneously, organically
produced but have in fact been produced by the imperative of

communication. Pornography moves from being understood as illicit, indecent materials which pose a challenge to contemporary mores and customs, to being just another vehicle for "honest" sexual expression for and by the masses.

This is not immediately apparent, however, since Internet distribution allows the consumer greater privacy. Paul takes increased privacy to be one of the central motivations for today's pornography user. She describes one of her interviewees: "He would never go out and buy a magazine or rent a movie. Since Zach and his friends grew up with the Internet, pornography was never about print or video. It's too big a hassle. You have to spend money. Somebody could find it lying around." And another one: "Watching with the guys was part of the problem. William doesn't like pornography to be so out in the open; he didn't want to witness other men masturbate. It's all well and good to enjoy porn on your own turf, but William has never rented a video himself or visited an adult theater because it gives him the creeps. 'Pornography has always been a private thing for me,' he explains" (2005, 26–27). However, she also mentions pornographic chat rooms and message boards, pointing to the ways in which Internet pornography is uniquely public. For Paul, this motivates consumers because it allows for male bonding and validation of masculinity. "An atmosphere of posturing and competition pervades such chat rooms. By commenting on women as a group, men keep women at a distance, parading their masculinity and proving their potency to one another, like roosters strutting their stuff in a barnyard competition" (37). Paul's analysis fails to underscore that the two factors—increased privacy and increased sharing—are logically related in conditions of democracy.

As pornography becomes more private (cheaper, faster, and easier to access discreetly than ever before), the pornographic imaginary becomes one of communities, networks of support, sharing, and open discussion. The paradox is only apparent. Commercial pornography consumption has always been a phenomenon of "the masses," but what happens when it imagines itself as such rather than as something individuals do in hiding? If pornography is a privileged exemplar of the democratic model, not one among others, it is no accident that more and more websites are devoted to free file sharing, where registered users upload and download videos, discuss them, and rank them, all of it organized according to a logic of democratization and information sharing. For instance, adultshare.livejournal.com describes itself as a "porn trading community," and broadcastyourass.com claims to be "the youtube of porn." This is true for sites on which users share professionally made "glossy" videos, as well as amateur sites where they upload their own, much less hi-tech creations. Do we not hear echoes of Lyotard in this account of a culture in which everything speaks, babbles, climaxes, in which the secret has disappeared and all femininity has been made visible? Of interest from this perspective is not whether pornography does in fact succeed in showing "it," but that it aims to in the first place. Borrowing from Baudrillard, we might call this phenomenon the *ecstasy of community*.

4   THE ECSTASY OF COMMUNITY

It could be argued that the sharing communities made possible by Internet distribution play an important strategic role in many liberationist projects, particularly those grounded in the idea of community. For example, Williams argues that the more countercultural the pornography, the greater its potential to resist heteropatriarchal normativity. The Internet has revolutionized pornography, she writes, by allowing for an unprecedented diversity of sexual identities and practices to assert themselves. The Internet, it seems, has the potential to queer pornography: "The 'diff'rent strokes' elicited by the pornographic genre's quest to see more, to know more, of the pleasure of the other turn out to be at odds with its attempts to subsume this pleasure within the terms of the reigning, but always fragile, 'normal' masculine heterosexual economy of desire" (1992, 240). Her analysis focuses on the contents of moving-image pornographies. The more diverse and "perverse" the narratives, she writes, the more difficult it is to describe all pornography as serving patriarchal ends.

What is striking about Internet pornography, however, in contrast to previous forms of hard-core moving-image pornography, is the metalevel discourse of information sharing in which it is situated. It is as if the Internet were uniquely equipped for pornography, in ways that print and film are not. There is something about the imaginary of democratized information that immediately makes it porn-friendly, or that at the very least makes people take off their clothes. Chat communities, for example, many of which do not overtly announce any sexual content, seem to immediately and spontaneously become places where men masturbate while chatting with women or men who are performing webcam shows for them. Get on chatroulette.com[1] and you will encounter an endless stream of penises in more or less erect states, because most male users have their cameras pointed directly at their genitalia. This is not to be confused with the dirty man flashing you in the park at night. This is a voluntary, noncommercial, mutual interaction in which women and men are watching their (male) interlocutors' real-time genital responses to what they're doing. Neither is it a form of phone sex, which is technologically mediated but nevertheless remains dyadic. Chatroulette's homepage shows exactly how many users are online at the very moment when one's specific, goal-oriented interaction takes place. Online, the more transgressive or extreme the depicted sex act is—or the more "other" the pornography, to borrow Williams's language—the more vibrant the fantasies of a countercultural community of misunderstood libertines who do not take their practices to be all that transgressive. And it is here that the logic of queering becomes complex and ambiguous. This metalevel presentation of the contents, rather than the contents themselves, is where Williams's queering hypothesis runs into trouble. In other words, it does not suffice to describe the diversity of practices asserting themselves if the mode of assertion is in unproductive tension with the resistant potential of the practices.

FILE SHARING: THE CASE OF BESTIALITY PORNOGRAPHY

Take the example of "zoo" or bestiality films, arguably quite far outside the mainstream of heterosexual pornography. Both feminist

critiques and the emerging field of porn studies are strangely silent
about it, proceeding as if the only ethically problematic commercial
porn production were that of child pornography and snuff films.
Responding in part to the emphasis placed by antiporn feminism
on ethical problems related to the conditions of porn *production*,
scholarship in porn studies often reorients the discussion toward
the conditions of *consumption* and the fact of pleasure, especially
women's pleasure. For instance, Williams writes that

> there is no commercial market for kiddie porn. If an occasional under-
> age performer is discovered, it is a source of great scandal and embar-
> rassment to the industry. And, despite all the hype, there is no snuff; nor
> does rape figure prominently in the narratives of recent pornography.
> Since pornography is about pleasure and aims to produce sexual plea-
> sure in its viewers, it is one of the few types of contemporary film narra-
> tive not to punish its female protagonists for seeking pleasure. (263)

I am not sure what to make of these claims, since in my own
research (limited to free sites) I found many rape sites. It suffices
to enter the rather unimaginative search phrase, "free rape mov-
ies," for instance. The claim about "kiddie porn" is a bit harder to
evaluate in the absence of empirical research, but I find it strange
that Williams does not mention the availability of virtual child
pornography, like "lolicon" *hentai*, still and animated cartoon
images of prepubescent girls, many of which are extremely violent. I understand that Williams refers to pornography depicting
real children, but her claim that there is no commercial market for
kiddie porn is misleading in light of the extensive hentai market.
And indeed, hentai shows the little girl "protagonists" experiencing pleasure, but it seems strange not to mention at this particular
moment that they experience pleasure as they are being raped by
tentacles and tortured. I understand Williams's reductive claim
that "pornography is about pleasure" to be a direct response to the
feminist claim that pornography is about sexual violence, but its
heavy-handedness is in direct conflict with all the nuances of her

work. A closer look immediately shows that there is never one thing that pornography is "about."

Even if the rape, kiddie, and snuff subgenres are slowly becoming extinct, the *production* of bestiality porn, which is widespread, clearly raises serious problems of agency, consent, and exploitation. Most zoo paysites show women having vaginal and oral sex with dogs and horses, occasionally inserting snakes, eels, or other fish into orifices. Many amateur, free sites also include films of men having intercourse with dogs, horses, cows, pigs, sheep, and so on, and the intercourse is not only vaginal but often anal (with men both giving and receiving), oral (ditto), and even with the sheaths of the penises of dogs. Not only do zoo sites show real humans performing real sex with real animals (as opposed to virtual pornography, which is the only form in which child pornography is easily accessible on the Internet), but they are also linked to websites about real-world bestiality practice.[2] They often piggyback on "information" sites about zoophilia, defined as love relationships with animals, usually to the exclusion of other humans and including sex. Although zoophilia websites openly condemn the use of animals in porn as "cruelty" and "exploitation," the porn sites' insistence that what they show is real ("100% real animal sex!!!") works to reinforce the connection. Bestiality is presented as something that must be kept secret, like the use of Internet pornography itself. Websites open in a sea of warnings, and the experience is that of entering ever deeper levels of something forbidden, when in fact there is nothing illegal about the viewing of most pornography, including bestiality pornography and virtual child pornography.

Simultaneously, because this imaginary is one of repression and the failure of society to understand the viewer's "needs," it is also of community, file sharing, and underground trafficking of information among users who form a network. Beastwiki.com, a site devoted to reviews of all of the bestiality paysites available, looks exactly like Wikipedia.com, except that the links are red and not blue. Sites like Zooshare.com are not only for file sharing but for posting blogs, commenting on posts, and reviewing the pornography, while users often describe themselves as keeping a secret, hiding their true selves, and being deeply misunderstood. Beastforum. com invites users to "share you opinions, creations, and experiences with others," and on the virtual zoo porn site Beasttoons. com, the female cartoon protagonist promises us an educational experience: "With your membership you'll also get full access to our extensive zoophilia database that covers everything you want to know about animal sex." Blogs are extensive in this scene, often including expressions of gratitude for the forum where open discussion can take place. While some blog posts discuss the considerable challenges of sharing one's desire for animal porn with a sex partner, others post about something very different, namely the difficulties of a life in which animals themselves are the sex "partners." This includes discussions about how to perform bestiality responsibly and in ways that do not harm the animals. The connection between bestiality pornography and bestiality practice is further reinforced by this imaginary of persecuted subculture, shared understanding, ethical concern, and results in creating a reality: a quasi-queer community that needs underground, democratic resources like the Internet in order to survive under conditions of legal repression and "straight" norms.

Surprisingly, the imperative to upload one's own porn occupies as important a place in porn-sharing communities as the pressure to pay for using the sites. Petsex.com, which advertises itself as "the world's largest bestiality and animal sex site," allows registered users to watch fifteen short films for free every day. The email sent to users upon first registration bears the subject line, "Welcome to the community." Whoever needs to watch more than fifteen films is then redirected to "upgrade," which is possible in one of two ways: either a paid membership or uploading one's own videos. In other words, by regularly adding one's own content, one indefinitely avoids paying. Again, the line between film-fiction and real practice becomes interestingly blurred as users imagine (correctly or not) that the films they watch not only are uploaded by other users but are in fact *by* those users or even *of* those users performing bestiality.

Furthermore, pornography sites are rife with rankings, a central feature of any online file-sharing community. Self-expression takes on even more layers: not only do users "show themselves"; they also show second-order information about the consumption of what is being shown (how many hits, when it was viewed most recently, and so on) and its reception (thumbs up or down, how many stars, member feedback, and the like). Some sites are devoted solely to ranking others:

> It seems like high quality rape porn is hard to find! With all the misleading links, deceptive ads and low quality rape content on the web, it's hard to find a site worth your time. But now, RAPE PAYSITE REVIEWS is here!! We give you a look of what's inside some of the best rape sites on the web. Find exactly what you need and enjoy nothing but the BEST! Visit Rape Paysite Reviews NOW and prepare to find the site you've always been looking for!! Let us guide you! (http://free.rapecore.com/)

According to Paul, the proliferation of rankings and public forums is simply masculine power expressed in the safest possible context, namely a world entirely devoid of women. The danger of this particular form of information exchange lies in the power it grants men over women, whose exclusion and objectification are at the heart of the maintenance of masculinity. "Women become objects to be praised, scorned, and sized up according to the degree to which they appeal to men. Such banter and debate may sound harmless, but it solidifies certain attitudes about the ease of judging a woman's merit solely on the basis of her appearance" (2005, 38). For Baudrillard, however, the problem with message boards and rankings has nothing to do with one social group enjoying power over another. Instead, the very terms of the practice, in which the information society is deluded into thinking that it is learning something about itself, are politically problematic. Something very specific is taking place when "the people enjoy day to day, like a home movie, the fluctuation of their own opinions in the daily opinion polls" ([1978] 2007, 60). To learn about itself, the subject must be split, divided, alienated from itself, seeing itself from afar, from outside, contradictory. But the information society with its opinion polls and sharing communities depends on the ultimate collapse of the social into itself, the loss of self-alienation, of distance and alterity. It can no longer learn anything about itself. Reality TV shows in which the viewing audience votes on who should continue on to the next "round" of talent competition (*American Idol*, *X Factor*, *Dancing With the Stars*, and so on) serve as proof of this. Such rankings

> exhibit this redundancy of the social, this sort of continual voyeurism of the group in relation to itself; it must at all times know what it wants, what it thinks, be told about its least needs, its least quivers, see itself continually on the videoscreen of statistics, constantly watch its own temperature chart, in a sort of hypochondriacal madness. The social becomes obsessed with itself; through this auto-information, this permanent auto-intoxication, it becomes its own vice, its own perversion. (1988, 210)

The ecstasy of community results in the social becoming self-obsessed and trapped in an (auto)erotic, self-referential, redundant circle.

Could it not be argued that porn sharing is resistant at its very core because it fundamentally alters the shape of the commercial pornography market, in precisely the same way that file sharing of music has irrevocably changed the music industry? In that sense, it seems, porn sharing and the growth of the amateur market have more viable and lasting effects on the commercial porn market than any legislation does. The public can affect the contents of pornography as both consumers and producers of pornography, putting certain subgenres and delivery methods out of business while causing others to thrive. According to this argument, the porn market is simply a direct expression of what the public wants, and it must change in response to social demands. However, the relationship between the product and the demand side of the industry is not so easy to articulate in causal terms. Paul insists, for instance, that the popular impression that pornography exists because it's what people want, or even what men want, is something like a mass hallucination, a large-scale consensual delusion, generated by the pornography itself. She blames Internet distribution in part for both this mass hallucination and the proliferation itself, stating that the Internet not only facilitates proliferation but in fact *fuels* it.

> Doubtless, the Internet has been a major driving force—perhaps the greatest force ever—behind the proliferation of porn. The kickoff may have been with a certain inadvertent combination of professionalism, celebrity, and amateurism. . . . In turn, the Internet's impact on pornography is practically a category unto itself. . . . The impact on market growth is astounding. You can pump out one statistic after another; the bulging numbers are almost mind-numbing. (59)

If it is true that Internet distribution causes more and more pornography to exist, what are the mechanisms that make this happen?

For Baudrillard, the problem is not that it is simply empirically false that men/people want pornography. The problem is, in a sense, more serious: in the age of information the public does not—and cannot—know what it wants. The information age changes the body politic from what he calls "the social" to what he calls "the masses." On this model, the communities formed around Internet pornography—even something as specialized and apparently marginal as zoo porn—function according to the logic of the "silent majority," silent because the imperative of communication produces no meanings. Baudrillard's mass is speechless, undifferentiated, precisely as it babbles and endlessly exhibits its manufactured diversity. "The mass is without attribute, predicate, quality, or reference. This is its definition, or its radical lack of definition. It has no sociological 'reality.' It has nothing to do with any *real* population, body, or specific social aggregate" ([1978] 2007, 38). Thus, pornography is problematic, not because a certain kind of image causes its consumer to commit a certain kind of act, or because this imagery produces gender-as-inequality, or that it distorts the truth of normal sexuality. It is problematic as an instrument of the kind of democracy that requires the disappearance of the secret existence and the autointoxication of the social. Given its success, Internet porn is arguably the most important tool of a social order which requires transparency of its subjects. Baudrillard writes in *Seduction*:

> We are living, in effect, amongst pure forms, in a radical obscenity, that is to say, in the visible, undifferentiated obscenity of figures that were once secret and discrete. The same is true of the social, which today rules in its pure—i.e., empty and obscene—form. . . . Shall we refer to Walter Benjamin's genealogy of the work of art and its destiny? At first, the work of art has the status of a *ritual* object, related to an ancestral form of cult. Next it takes on a cultural or *aesthetic* form in a system with fewer obligations; it still retains a singular character, though the latter is no longer immanent to the ritual object, but transcendental and individualized. Lastly, the aesthetic form gives way to a *political* form in which the work of art as such disappears before the inevitable progress of mechanical reproduction. If in the ritual form there are no originals (the aesthetic originality of cult objects is of little concern in the sacred), the original is again lost in the political form. There is only the multiplication of objects; the political form corresponding to the object's maximum circulation and minimum intensity. ([1979] 1990, 179–80)

Internet technology provides the ultimate fulfillment of the dream of mechanical reproduction: the loss of aura, the imagined loss of materiality, in the service of maximum iterability and circulation. The social consequences are great: "Through this feedback, this incessant anticipated accounting, the social loses its own scene. It no longer enacts itself; it has no more time to enact itself; it no longer occupies a particular space, public or political; it becomes confused with its own control screen." We enter the sphere of a politics without "scene," without alterity. "There is no longer any polarity between the one and the other in the mass. . . . This is what makes the circulation of meaning within the mass impossible: it is instantaneously dispersed, like atoms in a void. This is also what makes it impossible for the mass to be alienated, since neither one nor the other exist there any longer" (1988, 210).

I witnessed an example of what this means on the scale of mass consumption while watching British television, upon temporarily relocating to the United Kingdom in order to begin research for this book. The enormously popular vocal talent show *X Factor*, currently also on American television, allows the viewing public to vote for its favorite amateur singing contestant. The presence of a panel of judges ostensibly keeps the public in check, returning the discussion to questions of quality and talent, as opposed to other factors that might cloud judgment, like a contestant's likeability or "story." But during season 6 of the UK show, something strange happened, under the name "Jedward." John and Edward Grimes were seventeen-year-old identical twins about whom it was openly said in the media that they were completely devoid of any actual talent. Unable to successfully sing, rap, or dance, they were nicknamed "the vile twins" at the beginning of the season and yet remained in the contest for the UK's next pop phenomenon until close to the end, simply because of the public's continued support. They couldn't sing and they could barely dance, but their star just kept rising. The presence of the judges and their commentary on the quality of performances ultimately had no effect; at the end of the day, what mattered was whom the public chose. The "x factor" of the title, that mysterious thing called "star quality," remained unarticulated and determinable solely by the public vote. This shows how little it had to do with the questions of quality raised not only by the continuous feedback from the judges but by the twins' very presence. Ultimately, the "x factor" is completely coextensive with what the public wants. The public wants what it wants, or in short, it wants itself. The voting public is voting for itself in precisely the kind of vicious circle Baudrillard describes.

This, writes Baudrillard, is precisely what today's empty, "American" simulacral-democratic politics needs: "A speechless mass for every hollow spokesman without a past. Admirable conjunction, between those who have nothing to say, and the masses, who do not speak. . . . For some time now, the electoral game has been akin to TV game shows in the consciousness of the people" ([1978] 2007, 38, 59). Indeed, I suspect that the public's interest in the show (more than half of the British TV viewing public tuned in every Saturday night) has less to do with its interest in "talent" per se and more to do with a certain fascination with democracy at work. Part of the dramatic appeal of the show is precisely the *non*-correspondence between the judges and the public, of which Jedward was a spectacular case. The twins remained in the running not because the public was too stupid to realize that they lacked talent in fact. This was a case of the voters taking their power as voters and running with it, disqualifying more competent vocalists in the process and seeing how far this unfettered democratic process could go. But was this revolution, some kind of spontaneous mobilization of the people in the streets? Or was it instead a case of the masses obsessed with watching the results of their own votes on television, delighting not even in Jedward but in themselves? That the voting body was acutely aware of itself as democratic in this process was evident in Jedward's sudden appearance in a political campaign for the Labour Party at the time, which posted a photoshopped picture on its website with the faces of Conservatives David Cameron and George Osborne superimposed beneath John and Edward's blonde pompadours. The slogan reads, "You won't be laughing if they win."[3]

MASS AND CLASS

Kipnis might reject Baudrillard's critique of massification and references to "the extermination of meaning" ([1986] 1999, 10) as just another instance of the classist denigration of popular culture as "masturbatory." "Why do these motifs of masturbation and pornography make such frequent and highly publicized appearances in conservative arguments about culture? . . . It's indicative of just how much the canon needs pornography as the thing to mark its own elevation against" (Kipnis 1999, 182). Feminist discussions of pornography initially pointed critically to pornography's eroticization of the subordination of women, and later explored the eroticization of power difference in general. Kipnis departs from these kinds of moves, which makes her sophisticated analyses of pornography as a theater for class struggle so novel. She argues that (some) pornography forces uncomfortable confrontations with fat bodies, aging bodies, "disgusting" bodily excretions, and "dirty" humor, thematizing questions of taste and propriety, and thus, however unwittingly, enacting "the history of disgust as a mechanism of class distinction." She writes,

> Historically speaking, manners have a complicated history as a mechanism of class distinction, that is, of separating the high from the low. Implements we now take for granted, like the fork and the handkerchief, were initially seen as upper-class affectation (you both blew your nose into and ate with your hands, and from communal dishes). Only gradually did they filter down through the social hierarchy. But as money rather than aristocratic origins became the basis for social distinctions, manners took on an increasing importance, and they too started disseminating down through the population. Although originally mechanisms of social distinction, these behavior reforms and increasingly refined manners were also progressively restructuring internal standards of privacy, disgust, shame, and embarrassment throughout the population, thus transforming both daily and inner life. . . . The power of grossness is very simply its opposition to high culture and official culture, which feels the continual need to protect

itself against the debasement of the low (the lower classes, low culture, the lower body). (135–37)

At the same time that pornography presents misogyny, it also, in some cases, presents the voice of the disenfranchised speaking out against the upper classes, making the question of porn's political belonging ever more complex. In contrast to "*Playboy* and *Penthouse*, in which all women are willing and all men are studs—as long as its readers fantasize and identify upwards, with money, power, good looks, and consumer durables," pornography like *Hustler*, in which disgusting things play such a central role, acts as political speech speaking about class: "The fantasy life here is animated by cultural disempowerment in relation to a sexual caste system and a social class system" (151). Thus, Kipnis would agree that pornography invariably shows power differences, but not that it is a simple expression of male power over women: "The ways in which sex, gender, class, and power intersect in *Hustler* are complex, contradictory, and ambivalent, making it impossible to maintain that this is any simple exercise in male domination" (152).

Kipnis's work thus offers the most compelling critique of Baudrillard, who writes about pornography precisely in terms of mass consciousness. But Baudrillard is not just another bourgeois intellectual rejecting the "low." Moving the discussion around power from contents to form, or "delivery method," shifts our understanding of the relationship between sex and power to another level of abstraction. Baudrillard shows that what gets eroticized in the pornography proper to the age of communication and information is the disappearance of the real, the massification of the body politic. To understand the unique political effects of cyberporn, then, we must come to think about power not in terms of how pornographic materials depict power differences in their contents, but in the way that the delivery method that is the ecstasy of community constitutes a new kind of governable subject. Thus, while Kipnis is right that pornography depicts power differences along many axes and in complex ways, the way in which a text like *Hustler*, for instance, critically presents social power is less interesting to Baudrillard than the way in which it makes itself circulatable and reviewable. Furthermore, if we follow Baudrillard, MacKinnon and Dworkin's claim that pornography depicts something real (rape, violence) falls apart. The erotics of pornography according to Baudrillard depend instead on the suspension of the real and on the surrender to hyperreality and simulacrum.

Of all the strange claims in *America*, one sticks out in particular apropos the Marquis de Sade: "In 1989 the Revolutionary Olympic Games will be held in Los Angeles to mark the bicentenary of the French Revolution." This is false, of course, and curious, given that Baudrillard published his book in 1986, two years after the 1984 Olympic Games were held in Los Angeles and just as preparations were underway for the 1988 games in Seoul. Yet the claim concerns not historical fact but the idea that revolution is simply not possible in Baudrillard's America: "What would the promoters of the bicentenary do if a new revolution broke out between now and 1989? But there is no way that can happen" ([1986] 1999, 57). Accordingly, Baudrillard's claims are not about quality control, reorienting us from low back to high culture or class. The problem is not that the masses have decided to consume something of low quality or little significance but that the logic of massification suspends the issue of quality altogether, so that "low" and "high" no longer signify. Indeed, it is precisely in America that class is imagined to be fluid and easily transcended, nothing more than an Old World anachronism.

5 PRIVACY AND PLEASURE

Although any talk of women or gender is conspicuously absent from his critique of pornography, Baudrillard's consistent articulation of the silent majority as "America" locates him in proximity to some American antiporn feminism. MacKinnon and Dworkin have both argued that there is something about pornography that is distinctly American, though this point was never at the center of their critiques or articulated quite as strongly. In a passage that is strikingly similar to Baudrillard, for instance, Dworkin writes that sexual abuse (of which pornography production and consumption are both instances for her) is especially welcome and celebrated in "Amerika" (sic), which is a "landscape of forgetting." In this geopolitical imaginary she calls "Amerika" it is possible to forget everything from the genocides of indigenous people to institutionalized sexual abuse (see Dworkin 1997).

In a slightly different tone and far greater detail, MacKinnon draws connections between pornography and the culture of the First Amendment. She argues against the idea that pornography is an endangered speech that risks being suppressed by the state in the same way that communist publications were censored by the

U.S. government in the 1950s. On the contrary, she writes, it is in fact the perfect expression of the patriarchal state, a veritable instruction booklet (1993a, 112–13). It is the American speech par excellence, and so naturally the Supreme Court's job is to protect it at all costs, and to protect it under the uniquely American slogan, "freedom of speech." The trajectory from an American notion of freedom as freedom from government to pornography is direct and literal for MacKinnon. In the broadest-strokes-possible version of her argument, society is organized in terms of men's power over women; that power is maintained by the compulsory heterosexual sex act itself; freedom is conceived as the freedom to perform that act repetitively; women are defined by their status as objects for male pleasure; and pornography eroticizes objectification and subordination. Again, if we take America to be a sort of ideal, a model of modern liberal societies, pornography is not an accident of culture but essential to the functioning of America, where de jure liberalism cloaks de facto male supremacy. "Because sexuality arises in relations under male dominance, women are not the principal authors of its meanings. In the society we currently live in, the content I want to claim for sexuality is the gaze that constructs women as objects for male pleasure. I draw on pornography for its form and content" (1987, 53).

MacKinnon's critique of pornography qua instruction manual, however, depends too heavily on the contents of the images. One of its pitfalls is that it rests on the assumption that hard-core pornography *depicts* women in ways which hurt women as a group—either as sexually abused and hating it, or (more often) as sexually abused and loving it. When the discussion moves to the false representation of women's sexuality, it becomes possible to pose the following challenges: Does it follow that soft-core materials are less problematic than hard-core ones? And what about Williams's claims about "diff'rent strokes" for different folks, not just in terms of taste and sexual predilections but of a real need for community and political voice? What about "feminist" pornography for straight

women, and queer women's pornography, both of which are produced by women, target women consumers, and aim to contribute
to women's ongoing sexual liberation—like Candida Royalle's
Femme Productions and *On Our Backs* magazine? Or Deaf Bunny,
a company which specializes exclusively in hard-core porn by actors
fluent in American Sign Language? At this point, the debate turns
to differences of degree, as if some kinds of pornography were
potentially better than others, as we continue to analyze the images
themselves as a social semiotic which teaches men and women how
to look at women, how to perform gender, and how to approach
their bodies and sexual pleasure (however varied, dynamic, fluid,
and surprising the approaches may in fact be[1]).

But questions of contents cannot matter alone, abstracted from
questions of the method of delivery. If Internet pornography
emerges as the perfect manifestation of the babbling political body,
the speechless mass, in which every subject is interchangeable for
every other, exercising its rights and expressing, expressing, more
and more, telling us what we already know, climaxing, climaxing,
always recognizable and predictable, this has important consequences for feminist projects. And it is in her critique of American
privacy law, rather than of pornography itself, that MacKinnon
offers some conclusions closely related to Baudrillard's insight that
the effect of pornographic culture is to produce a particular kind
of body politic; and Lyotard's, that the babbling of democracy
leaves no room for saying anything real and that the pressure to
speak obliterates the secret. MacKinnon's work on the gendered
nature of privacy in the American legal imaginary intersects more
productively with the poststructuralist critique of the pornographic subjectivity than does any of her work on pornography.

What are rights exactly, and what would it mean to figure privacy as a right? The history of legal literature presents rights as
possessions, something we have, lose, fight for, and "hold."
Micheline Ishay, for instance, provides an extensive history of
human rights without once questioning the model that leads her

to begin the introduction with the claim that "human rights are held by individuals" (2004, 3). Iris Young's account of rights as something we do, rather than something we have, poses an intervention to the logic of rights as possessions accepted in legal literature. "Rights are relationships, not things; they are institutionally defined rules specifying what people can do in relation to one another. Rights refer to doing more than having, to social relationships that enable or constrain action" (1990, 25). In addition to this metalevel question of how rights should be conceived, privacy has never been merely one right among others. "Thinking about the notion of privacy forces us to confront fundamental issues at the heart of human rights. . . . If we trace the notion of the concept, we find that privacy is not a traditional constitutional right; one does not find 18th century revolutionary demands for privacy," writes legal theorist Andrew Clapham (2007, 108–9). Instead, we find the earliest invocations of a privacy "right" in late–nineteenth-century American legal cases and centered on unauthorized observation or publicity. The category of the private has been particularly significant for debates concerning women as subjects of rights, because the construction of the feminine as belonging properly to the private, domestic sphere has historically caused the exclusion of women from civil society. It has also been significant in debates concerning free speech (114).

Thus, Young's model of rights is more appropriate to an analysis of the particularly gendered nature of privacy. The right to privacy as formulated in the *Roe vs. Wade* decision is one emblematic example of how this right functions for women as a relationship that both enables and constrains action. The Supreme Court found that the criminalization of abortion was inconsistent with the constitutionally guaranteed right to privacy, and thus abortion was decriminalized and privatized in one and the same gesture. This gesture has been criticized considerably by feminist theorists[2] as one of the central rights dressed up as "human" but in fact excluding women in practice. Privacy understood as freedom from government allows existing patriarchal institutions and practices to continue uncompromised by government incursions and regulations. As MacKinnon puts it, privacy law "keeps some men out of the bedrooms of other men" (1987, 102).

Far beyond *Roe vs. Wade*, privacy as a negative freedom operates in international human rights documents concerning abortion. Human rights advocates interpret abortion law in terms of private decisions about one's reproductive capacity, calling on both the 1966 International Covenant on Civil and Political Rights (Article 17.1) and the American Convention on Human Rights (Article 11), which state that "No one shall be subjected to arbitrary or unlawful interference with his privacy, family, home or correspondence, nor to unlawful attacks on his honor and reputation" (n.d.). However, MacKinnon writes, while privacy is supposed to be a fundamental human right, in heteropatriarchal practice the law has protected the privacy of men at the expense of the privacy of women, shielding "the place of battery, marital rape, and women's exploited labor." Women themselves have no privacy, and this lack of privacy defines womanhood and the particular relationship of women to the domestic sphere. It is because the feminine is *exhaustively* defined by the domestic/private sphere—sexuality, childbearing and childrearing, domestic labor, caretaking, and so on—that the private sphere is "private" only for men. "Feminism confronts the fact that women have no privacy to lose or to guarantee" (1987, 101–2).

Kipnis attempts to reorient the controversy over pornography towards privacy, writing that "pornography is often cited, by antiporn feminists, as a causal factor in many bad things that happen to women. But the fact is, these domestic abuses depend completely on the protections of privacy . . . whereas pornography's impulse is in the reverse direction: toward exposure, toward making the private public and the hidden explicit" (1999, 172). She treats pornography and the protection of privacy as two separate potential causes of "bad things that happen to women." For

MacKinnon, however, the protection of "domestic" abuses and the protection of pornography happen in one and the same legal gesture: the protection of privacy. Pornography *is* one of those "bad things that happen to women" that the right to privacy protects. She points to an alternative, "positive" version of privacy, understood not as freedom from state incursions but as the kind of privacy that makes autonomy and self-definition possible at all (1987, 99–102). This is not a privacy that protects a preexisting interiority but the condition of the possibility of this interiority. Whether or not MacKinnon knows it, what follows from her critique of privacy is that the self does not preexist the conditions in which it begins to articulate itself. Although she is typically read as the great denier—of pleasure, speech, and most of all, women's sexual agency, as when Bell writes that "the blind spot in her theory is the possibility for female sexual agency in a sexist/racist/classist system" (1994, 83)—it is possible to distill her position down to three central moments, only of which one is negative/repressive while the other two remain positive/constructive:

1. The demand that pornography be seen as a form of sex discrimination, from which its legal repression would follow

2. The desire for full civic participation of women as women, not as ungendered "people"

3. Positive privacy

Unfortunately for MacKinnon, the three cannot coexist without serious inconsistencies. Strossen and Bell both claim that (1) and (2) are at odds with each other, arguing that legal constraints on pornography hurt women's chances, especially those of pornographic women (Bell's term), for full civic participation in the form of self-expressive and self-representing speech. In order to make these three claims consistent, the antiporn project must assume a different notion of speech than the one at work in Strossen and Bell's texts. And indeed, to make sense of the positive moments in MacKinnon's work (her demand for the positivity of privacy and of speech, which she claims women do not currently enjoy), we must bring in a model of speech that would not be shut down by legal repression of cyberporn (were such a thing practically possible, which is a separate issue). We must turn away from the cyberlibertarian model of speech as expressing preformed interior states of mind and for which "freedom" is synonymous with "coming out."

The kind of confessional speech that Butler prioritizes is fundamentally heterogeneous to the redundant babbling of the democratic masses under the pressure of the imperative of communication. It is transformative, surprising, unsettling, like the sexual itself. Sexuality is not properly speaking "mine" to "ex"-press. Butler's critique of identity politics rests on her fundamental skepticism towards any discourse in which description of a sexual category is mistaken for liberation of that sexuality (2004a, 121). "Coming out as a lesbian," for example, is hardly self-explanatory or simple, she writes:

> Who or what is it that is "out," made manifest and fully disclosed, if and when I reveal myself as a lesbian? What is it that is now known, anything? What remains permanently concealed by the very linguistic act that offers up the promise of a transparent revelation of sexuality? Can sexuality even remain sexuality once it submits to a criterion of transparency and disclosure or does it perhaps cease to be sexuality precisely when the semblance of full explicitness is achieved? (2004a, 122)

In his engagement with Augustine's *Confessions*, Lyotard, like Butler, takes on the complexity of the act of confessing the sexual. He describes the sexual precisely in terms opposed to the logic of successful mission (erection, climax) and truth (the showing of them) that pornography provides. "The endurance of the sexual is its *flaccidity*. It bends, it slips, it does not confront. . . . The sexual continuously surprises, takes from behind, works from the back. Upright resolutions, probity and the honest promise—the sexual lets all this go; it will pass" (2000, 18–19). This thing that is not frontal or honest—how is it to be told, represented, shown? Sexuality cannot but fundamentally alter the rules of speech, the terms of the telling.

From Butler's perspective, then, the connections that we often see in feminist texts, made more or less explicitly, between sexual pleasure and speech—both "mine," both liberated—are thus at the very least logically problematic, somehow missing the point that the sexual ends where full disclosure begins. In some accounts, pornography itself can function as a certain kind of legitimation of sexual expression, and even specifically female expression and pleasure. As we have seen, Williams reminds feminists that pornography is one of the few forms of film narrative in which women are not punished for seeking pleasure (1992, 263). Accordingly, first-person accounts of activist pornography workers often present a seamless trajectory from healthy and free expression of embodiment and sexual pleasure to the making of pornography, as in the following passage by celebrated porn star and self-proclaimed proporn feminist Nina Hartley:

> I am a direct product of the new thinking around sex of the late 1960s and early 1970s, reflected in that literature. I grew up believing that nudity was beautiful; that home childbirth and breastfeeding were the preferred way, that no sex was "sinful" or "dirty" or "perverse" if it was consensual, and that it was okay to be a dyke. *Our Bodies, Ourselves* said that consensual exhibitionism and voyeurism were not bad, but acceptable sexual variations. So in some ways, it was a natural progression for me to arrive at proud participation in the depiction of fucking and to explore that side of myself. (1997, 59–60)

In Hartley's account, pornography is nothing other than a "depiction of fucking," making the straight arrow of the narrative almost necessary. As Lyotard might ask (rhetorically), why wouldn't one go from simply having healthy, consensual sex in private to proudly showing it off to others?

This is the kind of feminism that Baudrillard rejects in *Seduction*, arguing that "there is a strange, fierce complicity" between feminism and the pornographic culture of telling the unrepressed "truth" of sex ([1979] 1990, 8). With its insistence on women's right to sexual pleasure, he writes, feminism is guilty of the same political mistake as porn: "The despoilment of the orgasm, the absence of sexual pleasure, is often advanced as characteristic of women's oppression. A flagrant injustice whose immediate rectification everyone must pursue in accord with the injunctions of a sort of long-distance race or sex rally. Sexual pleasure has become a requisite and a fundamental right. The most recent of the rights of man" (15). The insistence on the right to sexual pleasure conflates the feminine with the masculine as it reduces sex to orgasm, "a technological product of a machinery of bodies." (20). Pornography answers the feminist demand perfectly: "Henceforth women will climax, and will know why. *All femininity will be made visible*—woman as emblematic of orgasm, and orgasm as emblematic of sexuality. No more uncertainty, no more secrets." This is a story of the feminine "in a culture that produces everything, makes everything speak, everything babble, everything climax . . . at the expense of the female as a principle of uncertainty" (20). In fact, the kind of pornography produced by self-proclaimed feminist proporn activists like Hartley, whose merchandise today consists largely of instructional sex videos, is politically the most dangerous kind from Baudrillard's perspective.

UNPACKING "SEXUAL PLEASURE"

There are multiple axes of criticism at work here. The political point concerns the problems of figuring orgasm as a right. The epistemological point concerns the visibility and epistemological transparency of orgasm. I will begin with the latter because it is here that Baudrillard and Williams can confront each other in productive ways. For both of them, the "it" that (mainstream, heterosexual) pornography wants to show is the woman's pleasure, her orgasm. Williams bases her idea of the crisis of the visibility of pleasure on this, arguing that because women's orgasm is fundamentally fakeable (unlike men's, which may and therefore must be visually demonstrated), the "it" that pornography is after is never entirely, directly attainable. Thus, the so-called "money shot," in which the man pulls out and ejaculates visibly, ubiquitous in straight pornography, is readable in terms of what it does not show. She writes,

> The female body, for example, whose secrets of pleasure are especially solicited by the dominant mainstream of heterosexual pornography originally created for men only, tends, in the regime of the visible, to keep some of its secrets. . . . External ejaculation, while ideally visible and affording incontrovertible evidence of at least the male's pleasure, thus "perverts" "normal" genital aims. It is a substitute for the invisible female orgasm that this stage of the heterosexual pornographic genre especially solicits. . . . [The money shot provides] the spectacle of ejaculation as a substitute for what is not there: the invisible female orgasm. (1992, 241–43)

Williams argues that the female orgasm is "what is not there," and thus that pornography is more complex than an analysis like Baudrillard's allows.

For Baudrillard, the "mystery" of female pleasure is precisely what marks the feminine as veiling and artifice, and thus the maintenance of this mystery is absolutely essential to the logic of seduction.

> Uncertainty as to the female orgasm is at the heart of the sexual illusion. Whereas man is real, having to deal with the reality of his erection and hardly being able to simulate that effect (desire, for its part, can merely be virtual, but the erection is real)—woman is less linked to any reality whatsoever, except to that of her partner. She is, therefore, closer to illusion, play, and simulation. . . . Man and woman do

not have the same status of reality. But this is also the reason why there is no sexual relation. ([1997] 2007, 138)

Or rather, what sex is precisely not about is anything like "relation." Instead, "the very possibility of sexuality rests on the fact that each of us is ignorant of how the other comes (or even if). This is a vital misunderstanding, one could say. It's the biological form of the secret. . . . Fortunately, this is so, for this is how the woman can eternally seduce us, by means of this hidden jouissance, which thus becomes an incalculable pleasure." Baudrillard relates this essential mystery and incalculability of women's sexual pleasure to the sovereignty of the object. It marks woman's ontological impenetrability, her "absolute superiority over the man" ([1990] 2008, 158).

At first glance, Baudrillard's analysis of objectification and power appears contrary to feminist projects, but in fact it is only contrary to a very limited, liberal feminism in which the notion of sexual freedom is tied to subjectivity and agency, placing objectification on the side of unfreedom and oppression. "Therein lies the whole misunderstanding about sexual liberation," he writes, a misunderstanding that results in the leveling of true sexual difference, which does not properly take place between subjects ([1990] 2008, 159). For Baudrillard, the idea of power in the realm of sex is tied specifically to the object, not the subject. Sexual power is the power that the object has over the subject. Sex is not about orgasm, or even about relation, but about metamorphosis, which is possible only in conditions of radical sexual difference—not the difference between two subjects but that between subject and object. "Seduction alone can put an end to the domination of one sex over the other." The only way to speak of sex and power in the same register (which for Baudrillard is already problematic) is to realize that only the object has power, as it mirrors the subject's desire back to him and frustrates any possibility of intersubjectivity or relation. The object's power consists in its absolute inability to relate or to signify in any agential way. The object does not

produce meanings; it can only have meanings fetishistically projected onto it by the subject ([1990] 2008, 159–60). Here Baudrillard echoes Luce Irigaray's ([1977] 1985) critique of the West's
foreclosure of the possibility of female subjectivity. Like her, he
questions the possibility of anything like sexual "difference"
between women and men in conditions in which men create reality, or at the very least in which the masculine and the real are
ontologically related.

A feminism that includes how-to videos and pornography as
part of its mediation of a sexual relation between equals whose
secrets of pleasure can be made equally knowable and thus equally
achievable, a feminism that, in short, endows man and woman
with the same status of reality—this is the feminism Baudrillard
rejects as pornographic. Sex becomes pornographic as it turns the
secret of feminine pleasure into hard reality, like that of masculinity. Following Foucault in some sense (in spite of himself), Baudrillard would also bemoan pleasure coming into the service of
norms. The present feminist proporn culture is rife with this,
including instructional videos like "How to Female Ejaculate,"
starring Deborah Sundahl (n.d.) and Shannon Bell. "All women
have a prostate just as all men do. Therefore, all women can ejaculate," announces the commercial website.[3] As feminism commits
the crime of unveiling the mystery of female pleasure, pornography commits the worse—and related—crime of co-opting the
mystery qua mystery into its economy of utopian continuity: "It
is no accident that all pornography turns around the female sex.
This is because erections are never certain. . . . In a sexuality made
problematic by demands to prove and demonstrate itself without
discontinuity, the marked position, the masculine position, will
be fragile. By contrast, the female sex remains equal to itself in its
availability, in its chasm, in its degree zero" (Baudrillard [1979]
1990, 26).

For Williams, the money shot is the manifestation of anxieties
around female pleasure. It is because female pleasure is irreducibly

fakeable that the money shot is so important, an undeniable, spectacular substitute for female pleasure. The man's orgasm has no function but to relieve anxieties about the woman's. But Williams never asks why female pleasure is so important as to need this form of substitution in the first place. For Baudrillard, pornography functions productively, contributing to the creation and maintenance of a society in which so-called sexual liberation can be conceived of only as more and more sex, "a profusion come true, a 'sexually affluent society.' It can no more tolerate a scarcity of sexual goods than of material goods" ([1979] 1990, 26). Kipnis's analysis of pornography as a medium for a certain class consciousness is consistent with this:

> Perhaps the abundance of pornography—such an inherent aspect of the genre—resonates with a primary desire for plenitude, a desire for counter-scarcity economies in any number of registers: economic, emotional, sexual. Pornography proposes an economy of pleasure in which not only is there always enough, there's even more than you could possibly want. That has to have a certain grab to it, given the way that scarcity is the context and the buried threat of most of our existences, whatever form it takes—not enough love, sex, or money are favorite standbys. (202)

For Baudrillard, however, this desire for plenitude and abundance is what distinctly places the feminine at the center of the pornographic imagination. The mystery of female pleasure is pivotal to the genre precisely because "this utopian continuity and availability can only be incarnated by the female sex" ([1979] 1990, 26).

Finally, MacKinnon has a very different explanation for the compulsive need to ascertain female pleasure. In fact, to make a firm distinction between the politics and epistemology of female orgasm, as I have done, obscures the connection between them, a connection she takes to be at the center of male dominance. Williams and Baudrillard commit this mistake by taking the fundamental fakeability of female orgasm as given and natural, as if women's orgasms simply were invisible and therefore fakeable. MacKinnon, on the other hand, presents the social conditions that allow for this epistemological crisis around the female orgasm in the first place, showing that there is nothing given or obvious about it. When we begin from the assumption that women *can* fake orgasms, we fail to ask *why* women fake orgasms, or why anyone would fake sexual pleasure at all. The answer is obvious once we take seriously the idea that sex is a power relation: in a world in which men's power over women is manifested in the sex act, women's consent to men's power, or their own naturalization of their subordination, is their sexual pleasure at the hands of men. This creates a situation in which female orgasm is so (politically) necessary as to be in (epistemological) crisis at all times. "[Men's] Cartesian doubt is entirely justified: their power to force the world to be their way means that they're forever wondering what's really going on out there" (1987, 58). This phrase that is thrown around so casually, "women's sexual pleasure"—what is meant by it, how it functions socially, how it is represented and communicated—is thus a complex issue. Its relationship to pornography becomes even more complex when the pornography itself is packaged as being in the service of women's pleasure.

FROM .COM TO .ORG(ASM)

A recently published and widely disseminated statistic claims that approximately one in three visitors to adult entertainment websites is female. According to CNN, this information was discussed on the *Oprah Winfrey Show* and published in *O Magazine*.[4] In the spring of 2010, one of the best-known mainstream hard-core porn stars, Jenna Jameson, announced on one of the official websites of her production company that "porn is for girls, too! *Clubjenna. com* (as seen on Oprah)."[5] Reorienting the terms of the feminist discussion from the fact of women's degradation and harm to that of their pleasure is hardly an obvious or simple move. Baudrillard thematizes the stakes of this move in his first criticism of the relation between feminism and pornography. "Sexual pleasure has become a requisite and a fundamental right. The most recent of the rights of man" ([1979] 1990, 15). His point is not that women do not or should not experience sexual pleasure, but is directed at a particular way that feminism figures pleasure, namely in the language and logic of rights.

This connection has a rich history, which Lynne Segal details in *Straight Sex: Rethinking the Politics of Pleasure*. Women's liberation ideology of the late 1960s and early 1970s in the United States focused on the liberation of a unitary, repressed female sexuality as essential to its project. The way to a woman's autonomy and agency was through her clitoris, as it were, which was offered as proof that women's sexuality was essentially the same as men's. Precisely because sexuality was the site where women's material and political subordination were naturalized most easily, the trajectory from equality of sexualities to equality of rights appeared necessary (1994, 31–44). Today this discourse survives in the liberal feminism at work in much propornography literature, which is actually often directly at odds with the critiques present in contemporary feminist theory, where concepts like equality, rights, pleasure, and sexuality (as a category of analysis) come under close scrutiny.

Invocations of equality show up in texts such as Strossen's, which argues that the suppression of pornography threatens equality rights, never questioning the value of the concept of equality for women and sexual minorities. But this brand of feminism also fuels texts like Nina Hartley's website, Nina.com, where the emphasis on instructional sex videos and on the joys and freedoms that come with sexual expression indicates that civic participation in general concerns not speech but pleasure. Anniesprinkle.org(asm), for instance, is a site registered in the ".org" language of nonprofits rather than ".com" commercial websites, where there is no discontinuity between Annie Sprinkle's campaign to teach women how to orgasm more and her interest in raising ecological awareness. Sprinkle herself, "the first porn star to earn a Ph.D.," provides lecture tours about the "ecosexual" movement. Candida Royalle, former porn star and creator and director of Femme Productions, a line of porn films marketed to women and couples, announces on her site that she is the author of the introduction to a collection of women's erotica, the proceeds of which go to benefit Haitian women after the great earthquake of 2010 (www.candidaroyalle.com). Both Royalle and Sprinkle market themselves as educators and even healers. Is it not possible to read this as a Foucauldian moment in feminism, where pleasure is precisely that which cannot be normalized and thus may become the site of resistance? On Foucault's model, the connection between sexual pleasure and political speech and action appears necessary. But this reading works only on a certain model of the political, one that does not reduce the political to civic participation or democratic "expression," or pleasure to that which may be normalized and shown.

In the spring of 2010, Hartley announced on the homepage of her website her upcoming performance in Eve Ensler's play *The Vagina Monologues*. Proceeds from ticket sales "raise money and awareness of violence against women. This year's productions are benefitting the women and girls of Democratic Republic of Congo."[6] To the far right of the text was a vertical line of thumbnails advertising different films one can stream live (for a price) on the website, and the thumbs changed with each visit to the site. They included the films *White Boy Slam* (in which five white men have sex with one black woman), *Just Turned 18*, *Evil Anal* (featuring "more gorgeous sluts that love it in the ass"), and *Tough Love 13* (in which two "sluts" receive the "punishment" they "love" from two men, in the form of everything from having their hair pulled and getting their faces slapped by penises, to having their tongues pierced on the spot before a session of anal "punishment" intercourse). How are the two discourses related to each other— the pornographic one, comprised of fictions that depend on the erotics of violence performed on "masochistic" women, and the humanitarian one of raising awareness of real, nonfictional sexual violence against women in the Congo? How does ".org" so seamlessly become ".org(asm)" simultaneously with feminist consciousness raising?

Ensler herself has taken an active interest in Congolese women, traveling there and writing about victims of genocidal rape, and the hospital that treats them, for *Glamour* magazine. Her 2007 article "Women Left for Dead—and the Man Who's Saving Them"[7] includes graphic descriptions like the following:

> Dr. Mukwege tells me I need to meet Alfonsine (her name also has been changed). "Her story really touched me," he says. "Her body, her case is the worst I have ever seen, but she has given us all courage." Alfonsine is thin and poised, profoundly calm. She tells me she was walking through the forest when she encountered a lone soldier. "He followed me and then forced me to lie down. He said he would kill me. I struggled with him hard; it went on for a long time. Then he went for his rifle, pressed it on the outside of my vagina and shot his entire cartridge into me. I just heard the voice of bullets. My clothes were glued to me with blood. I passed out.[8]

Given that these are the kinds of things one learns in the course of having one's awareness raised about the Congo, it seems reasonable to wonder how the humanitarian discourse "works" as part of an active, bona fide commercial porn website. The raped Congolese women and the "sluts" in the films for sale on Nina.com are both discursive constructs framed by a complex and dynamic context which integrates claims about women's pleasure, systemic misogynistic violence, access to information, feminist identity and sisterhood, and personal testimony. It is neither accidental nor rare that these constructs appear side by side in the cultural production of propornography activists such as Hartley, Royalle, and Sprinkle, who take their own task, namely protecting pornographic materials from censorship while simultaneously increasing awareness about women's sexual pleasure, to be part and parcel of a broader campaign for protection of the human rights of women. Echoing Baudrillard, but reversing his critical spin, porn defender Wendy McElroy argues that pornography and feminism are actually motivated by the same liberationist need: "Pornography benefits women politically in many ways. Historically, pornography and feminism have been fellow travelers and natural allies. Although it is not possible to draw a cause-and-effect relationship between the rise of pornography and that of feminism, they both demand the same social conditions—namely, sexual freedom" (2004).

6 FORECLOSURE AND ITS CRITICS

Williams writes that "feminist debates about whether pornography should exist at all have paled before the simple fact that still and moving-image pornographies have become fully recognizable fixtures of popular culture" (2004, 1). Indeed, Williams's work relies on the very fact of pornography's existence, its tenacity in the face of legal repression and regulation, to make the point that it is undeniably a tool of and for the people. However, the mere fact of its existence and commercial success hardly shuts down the debate concerning the political belonging of pornography. Furthermore, what becomes clear as we take seriously the role of the Internet in the maintenance of this existence is that insisting on the connection between the pornographic and the people, as distinct from the state, becomes less satisfying in a context in which the people and the state are no longer easily distinguishable.

It is not difficult to construct pornography as politically significant: as labor; as gendered labor; as imagery which participates in gender production in a unique and powerful way; as imagery which eroticizes power difference along lines of gender, race, sexuality, ability, age, class, nationality, and as we have seen, even species, that

82

is precisely those axes of difference which politics is endlessly navigating; and as labor which depends on those power differences manifesting themselves in economic terms. It is irreducibly politically significant as sex, if we take seriously the feminist lesson that sex—all sex—is never not political. However, as Butler's analysis shows, this last claim is already too simple: the political itself is a field of productive tension between two incommensurable ways of relating to sexuality. On one hand, sexuality may be figured as intelligible, representable, and either legitimate (heterosexual, monogamous, age-appropriate unions, for instance) or not (gay and lesbian monogamous unions, for instance, or heterosexual polygamy in some religious contexts). On the other, it may function as unintelligible, unrepresentable, and outside the very possibility of legitimation, as in the case of more fluid, queer, and some trans- identities, or polyamorous kinship structures which do not seek legitimation by the state. These two poles are not in a relationship of symmetry, because the first is always privileged as recognizably political, in forms like "civic participation," while the second is often accused of apoliticality.

> Why, under the present conditions, does the very prospect of "becoming political" depend on our ability to operate within that discursively instituted binary and not to ask, and endeavor not to know, that the sexual field is forcibly constricted through accepting those terms? . . . To become political, to act and speak in ways that are recognizably political, is to rely on a foreclosure of the very political field that is not subject to political scrutiny. Without the critical perspective, politics relies fundamentally on an unknowingness—and depoliticization—of the very relations of force by which its own field of operation is instituted. (2004b, 107)

Butler would reject articulating sexual pleasure and sexual practice in terms of the language of rights because legitimation by the state effects what she calls "foreclosure." In fact, both legitimate and illegitimate sexual relations, which exist always in relation to each other, effect the "foreclosure of the sexual field" by stabilizing practices and meanings in relation to legal and social intelligibility. In Lyotard's terms, foreclosure means the impossibility of the event, or conditions in which "everything that is to be done is as if it were already done" ([1993] 1997a, 8). But the sexual field, she writes, is precisely the thing that cannot be foreclosed, schematized a priori and thus stabilized, if it is to be the site of freedom and resistance that we wish it to be in feminist and especially radical queer politics. "Why would we have the right to freedom of expression if we had nothing to say but the already said?" asks Lyotard, pointing to the need for protection of the secret existence on which any claim to human rights is based ([1993] 1997b, 121). For Butler, the sexual field is what Lyotard calls the "no-man's land" which makes thinking possible.

> We misunderstand the sexual field if we consider that the legitimate and illegitimate appear to exhaust its immanent possibilities. There is outside the struggle between the legitimate and the illegitimate— which has as its goal the conversion of the illegitimate into the legitimate—a field that is less thinkable, one not figured in light of its convertibility into legitimacy. This is a field outside the disjunction of illegitimate and legitimate; it is not yet thought as a domain, a sphere, a field; it is not yet either legitimate or illegitimate, has not been thought through in the explicit discourse of legitimacy. Indeed, this would be a sexual field that does not have legitimacy as a point of reference, its ultimate desire. (2004b, 105–6)

This site "at the limit of the intelligible" is where sex can become transformative and "critical" (107). The feminist insight that sex is political means a specific thing in Butler's analysis: when the sexual field is foreclosed, so is the political field, although this moment is precisely the moment when our claims become culturally intelligible as "political."

If what pornography does is legitimate female sexual pleasure as a right, as Baudrillard fears, then his account of pleasure made visible and intelligible, stabilized, determined a priori is an account of foreclosure. It will not suffice then to show that pornography as a cultural product is somehow invested in or committed to female sexual pleasure. *This fact alone does not make the discourses and practices involved progressive or transformative.* On the contrary: if orgasm = right, and subjectivity = sexual agency, how can we begin to think critically about, for instance, the hardcore heterosexual pornography niche called "forced female orgasm," in which women are tied down by male "captors" and ostensibly "tortured" with orgasms which last for as long as thirty minutes sometimes, in various scenarios of bondage and sadomasochism (for instance, hogtied.com)? Connections between human rights and rationality and discursivity are also operative here. If orgasm is a right and the subject of rights is the discursive subject, what emerges is a picture of sexual liberation in which orgasm = speech. Freedom of speech becomes guaranteed by money shots, and female ejaculate becomes the new money shot as "squirting" becomes an increasingly popular niche market.

Theorizing the progressive potential of pornography requires a different model of the political field than the one in which the notion of rights presently functions, as well as a different model of pleasure than the one presently at work in proporn feminist discourse. Butler provides a model of progressive sexuality as nonidentity, sites of unintelligibility from which different kinds of claims may be made:

> These are not precisely places where one can choose to hang out, subject positions one might opt to occupy. These are nonplaces in which one finds oneself in spite of oneself; indeed, these are nonplaces where recognition, including self-recognition, proves precarious if not elusive, in spite of one's best efforts to be a subject in some sense. They are not sites of enunciation, but shifts in the topography from which a questionably audible claim emerges: the claim of the not-yet-subject and the nearly recognizable. (2004b, 108)

From Butler's perspective, then, the problem concerns not whether the state should ban or sanction pornographic materials but the way in which the drive to legitimation compromises the capacity of any speech, including pornography, to be truly critical. The drive to protect citizens from hate speech by appealing to the idea that hate speech "shuts down" the speech of those subjugated by the representations, she argues, potentially repeats the very practices of exclusion and abjection which found the state, the practices which establish criteria of universality and speakability. In their turn to the state for help, defenses of pornography and calls for censorship alike suffer from the same failure to interrogate those criteria (Butler 1997). Intervention of the kind Butler calls for from queer speech and practice cannot be legitimated by the state.

Thus, protecting pornography and our rights to it is no more in line with a liberationist project involving critical sexuality than are bans or legal constraints on pornography. Butler, Baudrillard, and Lyotard belong to an intellectual tradition in which freedoms and real speech (in the sense of intervention) are structurally heterogeneous to the system, which cannot see them or think them, and so cannot sanction, enable, or protect them. The secret Lyotard and Baudrillard wish to save from extinction is always outside the law, beyond the reach of the state, and no civil or criminal legislation can properly protect it. Thus, no demand that a repression of pornography take place at the level of the law (criminal or civil) can yield it. Likewise, Butler's critical sexuality, just outside of intelligibility and subject-hood, cannot come about as a result of any kind of legislative legitimation *or* repression.

A concrete example might prove instructive here. The documentary film *Live Nude Girls Unite* (1999) chronicles the attempts of a group of professional nude dancers to unionize the peepshow theater in which they work, the Lusty Lady in San Francisco. After a long and involved legal battle, the Lusty Lady became the first unionized exotic dance theater in the United States. In one scene, the workers are on strike outside the club during the day in response to a fellow dancer getting fired for her unionizing activities. Picketing, they chant "2-4-6-8 / Don't come here to masturbate!" One of the regular customers, a handsome young man stopping by after work, finds the dancers on strike and speaks into the camera in support of their efforts as workers and citizens. He loudly and passionately encourages other customers to boycott the club until the women's demands are met. One of the dancers then enters the frame and flirtaciously promises him an extra good time when he next comes in, in gratitude for his support of their legal and ideological struggle. He nods enthusiastically. Both beam—at each other and the camera.

The legitimation of the dancer's citizenship in the greater community and demands for workplace equality, a legitimation effected of the language of labor and political organization itself, somehow manages to present the customers and the dancers as belonging to the same side, collectively organized against a common enemy. Both the dancer and the customer are laborers, after all. The film registers no inconsistency from one moment, when the customer declares his allegiance with the dancers, to the next, when we are reminded that he is in fact on the demand side of an industry in which the exploitation of workers is not only rampant but also (relatedly) justifiable in the legal and social imaginary. On the contrary, not only is there no inconsistency, but his boycotting activities will be rewarded with an extra good orgasm the next time he does in fact go to the Lusty Lady to masturbate. That these two subject positions can signify simultaneously in the figure of the male customer is an effect of the dancers becoming intelligible within a certain discourse of legitimation. Being seen as worthy of protection and privacy, of being heard by the state at all, is contingent upon their capacity to be made culturally, sexually, legally intelligible. Butler would argue that this comes at a serious price: we foreclose the possibility of metalevel questioning concerning the nature of the political itself.

On the other side of the debate, however, attacks on pornography usually rely on the same logic of legitimation. The Anti-Pornography Civil Rights Ordinance, proposed by Dworkin and MacKinnon in 1983, for example, proposes to treat porn as a violation of the civil rights of women and allows women who can demonstrate that porn has caused them harm to seek civil prosecution. "Pornography is thus defined as a form of discrimination and makes the following practices actionable: (i) discrimination by trafficking in pornography; (ii) coercion into pornographic performances; (iii) forcing pornography on a person; and (iv) assault or attack due to pornography" (Mason-Grant 2004, 162). There is a clear shift in focus from production to consumption as we go down the list of actionable practices. The ordinance tries to take seriously the idea that pornography may have harmful effects beyond just the conditions of production, in which the contents of the pornography are not at all at stake. It speaks precisely of contents and their social and material effects, and thus, predictably, it was found to violate the First Amendment. However, the focus on freedom of speech distracts from the details of the language in which the political subject herself is figured. The first section of the statement of policy begins, "Pornography is a practice of sex discrimination. It exists in [place], threatening the health, safety, peace, welfare, and equality of citizens in our community. Existing laws are inadequate to solve these problems in [place]," and later concludes that porn undermines "women's equal exercise of rights to speech and action guaranteed to all citizens under the [Constitutions] and [laws] of [place]" (Dworkin and MacKinnon, 1983). As it figures woman as a legitimate citizen whose rights, equality, and full belonging in "our community" are violated by this controversial cultural practice, the regulation or legal constraining of pornography necessarily involves foreclosure.

To be clear: my point is not that there ought to be no state regulation or repression of pornography. I hesitate to position myself at all regarding state regulation in this book. Neither does the critique of the notion that sexual pleasure is a right commit us to the position that women should not expect sexual pleasure in their lives or relationships. But if Butler is correct, then neither of these will—or, structurally speaking, can—guarantee the kind of paradigm shift in the figuring of the political subject called for by Baudrillard's and Lyotard's secrecy, as well as MacKinnon's privacy. These can only be thought, articulated, moved along from the critical perspective. "By recommending that we become critical, that we risk criticality, in thinking about how the sexual field is constituted, I do not mean to suggest that we could or should occupy an atopical elsewhere, undelimited, radically free. . . . One gets there, as it were, through suffering the dehiscence, the breakup, of the ground itself" (Butler 2004b, 107–8). The imperative to instability of meaning among these thinkers remains steadily Foucauldian. As Oksala writes about feminist emancipation, "it requires not a body pure of cultural constitution, but one that is constituted in ways that are open to reinterpretation and multiple meanings" (2005, 153).

The greatest difference between the (let's call it) Francophone critique I have been articulating and the distinctly "American" feminism of MacKinnon concerns the relationship between sex and the law. Vigilant critic of the law, MacKinnon nevertheless still has a certain faith in the power of the state to create conditions of greater freedom, like guaranteeing the kind of robust notion of privacy for which she calls. But those aspects of her work that most often earn her the label "radical" and that come under such fire from other feminists, I propose, are precisely what makes MacKinnon more relevant than ever to a critical understanding of Internet porn (Grebowicz 2011). Her work, too, introduces possibilities for refiguring the political field and for theorizing a sort of dehiscence. Of the American feminists of her generation, it is she who argues most rigorously against a particularly American liberal version of equality, which allows for the "separate but equal" treatment of women. The problem inheres in the very logic of gender, she writes, a logic which states that women are both naturally different from men and worthy of equality. The difference-and-equality approach results in women being treated more and more equally to men only when they are figured as less and less "different" from them. In response to this, MacKinnon argues that the two concepts are mutually exclusive: if we wish to hold on to the difference claim, we must surrender the claim to equality. If we desire equality, on the other hand, we must give up difference (1987, 36–37).

She chooses the first of these—sacrificing arguments for equality. This is what earns her the title "radical" against the backdrop of most American feminism, and simultaneously what makes MacKinnon's work relevant to contemporary critiques of the political. Despite their obvious differences, then, both MacKinnon and Butler would follow Baudrillard in his critique of the language of rights in feminist explorations of pleasure. More importantly, they would do so for related reasons. MacKinnon's critics who accuse her of precluding the possibility of women's agency, and especially women's sexual agency, are correct. However, read in the following way, this turns out to be not a flaw in her logic but a strategic move which aligns her with postmodern developments of the politics of the object, the abject, and the inhuman.

WHY MACKINNON MATTERS (AGAIN)

Since the early 1990s, feminist political thought has remained actively critical of human rights discourse (Gallagher 1997, 283). Early critiques stated that the category "human" disappears gender; in other words, that in spite of the de jure recognition of women, human rights documents and conventions suffer from a de facto androcentrism, and thus erase women as a group. In her work on international human rights, MacKinnon focuses on hyperfeminized women in order to undo this disappearing. She argues that when violence is wielded almost exclusively against women, and not against men, that violence is figured not as a human rights violation. It is the fact that something happens to women and not to men that makes it *not* a human rights issue. For example, sexual murder is considered a human rights issue only insofar as it is murder and thus deprives a gender-neutral subject of its life; but insofar as it is sexual murder—of which primarily women are victims—it is no longer a human rights issue but an issue of something like "women's rights." This is why, for instance, international human rights discourse cannot formulate a policy on sexual murder as something qualitatively distinct from murder, and genocidal rape as something distinct from both murder and rape, or even the concept of genocidal rape as a war atrocity (see MacKinnon 1993b); and why sexual and reproductive health rights are subsumed under the category "health rights" (Clapham 2007, 132). Human rights discourse "sees" women only insofar as they are stripped of the concerns proper to them as a social group. MacKinnon writes, "For women, international human rights presents the biggest gap between principle and practice in the known legal world" (1993b, 97).

She argues, as we have seen, that so-called natural differences between the sexes are produced by power difference. Women and men are not different "before" patriarchy, MacKinnon writes, but patriarchal logic depends on the difference claim. Since the difference-and-equality approach results in women being treated more equally to men only when they are able to be less different from them, much of her work focuses on what happens to women in the eyes of the law when they are the least situated like men. When women are at their most "feminine" in the sense of being feminized, othered in an androcentric legal order and social imaginary—as prostitutes, porn workers, domestic workers, incest victims, rape victims, subjects of abortions—their claims to equality necessarily fail. Andrea Dworkin's later work demands that feminists "remember" the women who are excluded every time we celebrate a public-sphere victory like voting rights or labor reform, excluded because the particular rights and protections they need are of the order of the private:

> The women's movement has to refuse to exile women who have on them the stench of sexual abuse, the smell, the stigma, the sign. We need to refuse to exile women who have been hurt more than once: raped many times; beaten many times; not nice, not respectable; don't have nice homes. There is no women's movement if it does not include the women who are being hurt and the women who have the least. . . . I'm going to ask you to remember the prostituted, the homeless, the battered, the raped, the tortured, the murdered, the raped-then-murdered, the murdered-then-raped; and I am going to ask you to remember the photographed, the ones that any or all of the above happened to and it was photographed and now the photographs are for sale in our free countries. (1995; and see MacKinnon 1993b and 1987, 85–92)

Thus, for instance, MacKinnon would argue that all murders of women at the hands of men, especially men they know, are sexual, regardless of whether or not rape or commercial sex took place. While the law demands a sameness with men in order for women's "human" rights to be protected, in practice the feminization of women makes the violences they suffer under patriarchy precisely not "the same" as those that men suffer, violences whose aim is often to precisely maintain feminization as a form of subordination.

This is why MacKinnon's tendency to rely so heavily on personal testimony is misleading in one important sense. While her work appears to be focused on actual women and the material conditions of their bodies and lives, what she is really concerned with is exposing a certain logic of domination, those legal and ontological conceptions of the feminine which allow for qualitative differences *among* women from the point of view of human rights. Human rights discourse accommodates those women who are situated most like men. The abject women—who are at the same time the most feminized women—are excluded from the category "human" when those systemic violences that affect them in particular are constructed as women's rights violations. This is because the subject of rights is constructed as public, and thus violence committed in the private sphere is rendered invisible. "The structure of international human rights law effectively excludes actions occurring in the private sphere and violations which are occasioned by non-state actors. This gendered construct ignores the fact that the vast majority of women live their lives firmly removed from the public domain" (Gallagher, 290). MacKinnon would add that even as women enter the public domain in ever greater numbers and in ever more contexts, the de facto construction of femininity as proper to the private sphere allows for a figuring of the subject of human rights which excludes the feminine in principle.

Thus, she argues, inclusion in the category "human" is impossible as long as we continue to define women as different, or as not-men. Rather than giving up difference, however, it is possible to refigure difference, as some poststructuralist political thinkers have done in their critiques of the human rights system (see Rancière 2004; and Lyotard 1993, [1993] 1997b, [1993] 1997c). Instead of giving up the difference claim, one may reject the category "human" and put difference at the center of the ontology of the subject of rights. This is what MacKinnon calls for, because recognizing the humanity of women does not guarantee the protection of their rights in a social order where some humans dominate others. On the contrary, "equal treatment of persons in unequal situations will invariably operate to perpetuate rather than to eradicate injustices" (Gallagher, 290). As MacKinnon puts it, "If society gives you no rights, such that a state need never deny them to keep you from having them, it may do little good to have them formally guaranteed in international law" (1993b, 98).

Rather than gesturing towards equality, neutrality, and state protection, MacKinnon thinks the subject of rights along the lines of the most abject and "outside." This makes possible not a re-articulation of the human as subject of rights to *include* the woman as subject of rights, but a re-articulation of the human to include the inhuman, the exiled, mute, opaque thing which is not subject to any rights, which constitutes its conceptual limit, exposing its contingency. At this point, the verb "to include" must fall away, because the inhuman is a sort of interruption, a demand, something which cannot be "included," which cannot really "be." "Thing" is a technical term for Lyotard. To refer to persons as "things," in this case, is to thematize the fact that outside of certain political discourses, we cannot properly call them "persons" or "human." Thus, the thing is precisely that which resists politics. But Lyotard calls for a thinking of "the political," as opposed to politics, in which the "thing" would not be forgotten.

The word "abject" is mostly associated with the work of Julia Kristeva, who uses it to refer to the breakdown in meaning caused by encountering "the jettisoned object, [which] is radically excluded and draws me toward the place where meaning collapses" ([1980] 1982, 2). Her examples of jettisoned objects are the corpse, shit, the open wound, but also certain encounters with food that provoke vomiting, retching, violent physical reactions of turning away from the abject thing. More abstractly, even actions and crimes function as abject if they are sufficiently "unthinkable."

> It is thus not lack of cleanliness or health that causes abjection but what disturbs identity, system, order. What does not respect borders, positions, rules. The in-between, the ambiguous, the composite. The traitor, the liar, the criminal with a good conscience, the shameless rapist, the killer who claims he is a savior. . . . Any crime, because it draws attention to the fragility of the law, is abject, but premeditated crime, cunning murder, hypocritical revenge are even more so because they heighten the display of such fragility. (4)

Like Ensler's encounter with the Congolese rape victims at their most vulnerable moments, the abject situates me in a particular ethical and epistemological crisis, in which I face something which is "not me. Not that. But not nothing, either. A 'something' that I do not recognize as a thing. A weight of meaninglessness, about which there is nothing insignificant, and which crushes me" (2).

In Butler's work the abject becomes a sort of non-subject-position from which to think resistance. The cultural unintelligibility of some marginalized sexualities becomes the very place from which to resist, rather than from identity and authenticity. "Oppression works not merely through acts of overt prohibition, but covertly, through the constitution of viable subjects and through the corollary constitution of a domain of unviable (un) subjects—*abjects*, we might call them—who are neither named nor prohibited within the economy of the law. Here oppression works through the production of a domain of unthinkability and unnameability" (2006, 126). "Abject" in this sense means outside "the thinkable, the imaginable, that grid of cultural intelligibility that regulates the real and the nameable."[1]

Some have criticized MacKinnon's work on the grounds that it focuses on the abjectitude of some sex workers to the exclusion of those sex workers who claim to enjoy their work and life. She is Bell's privileged example of "modernist feminism," which encloses "the prostitute body within a theorized totality which leaves no space for the prostitute herself as speaking subject" (1994, 187). This claim is problematic since so much of the modernist feminism Bell dismisses in fact relies heavily on testimony from sex workers. Perhaps the most publicized is that of *Deep Throat* actress Linda "Lovelace" Marchiano in Dworkin and MacKinnon's anti-porn campaign (Lasar 1995, 196). But Bell's more nuanced criticism is well taken: rather than showing a wide spectrum of sex worker experiences, ranging from the most "positive" and agential to the most exploited, MacKinnon presents only one kind of sex worker experience, just as she presents only one kind of effect of pornography on the lives of all women.

It has become commonplace in feminism to dismiss this focus on abjectitude, as well as many of MacKinnon's other substantive points, as rhetoric, as Lynne Segal does when writing about her "doomladen theatricality" (1994, 280). At stake is precisely the question of how the sex worker is figured. In Dworkin and MacKinnon's presentations before the Attorney General's Commission on Pornography in 1985, the emphasis on women as "agencyless victims—helpless hostages to male behavior" (Lasar, 194) aligned neatly with conservative responses to porn as "degrading" to women, a social vice from which femininity needed saving (Vance 1992, 34). Segal writes that MacKinnon and Dworkin "manipulate women's fears of male violence to make their own dangerous alliances with the anti-feminist Right, promising to 'rescue' women from pornography and the rapaciousness they think intrinsic to all men's heterosexual practice" (Segal, 280–81). The problem of complicity with the Right is not new: critiques of sex work and sexual materials have always taken place between feminists and conservative moralists simultaneously, and feminism has had to make continuous disclaimers in attempts to remove itself from this unholy alliance since the nineteenth century. The resonance often concerned precisely the "image" of the prostitute that each discourse offered up: was she poor, desperate, vulnerable to disease, hurt; or was she the ultimate figure of freedom and sexual agency?

Feminists focused on the former have always, and continue to, run the risk of being labeled sexual conservatives, as in Bell's offhanded remark about Carole Pateman's analysis of the increase in consumption of porn featuring fellatio (see Chapter 3). Pateman wonders if the increase in the consumption of this imagery might be a sign of antifeminist backlash at a time of the "revitalization" of "women's demand to speak." Bell reads the passage as betraying "the nature of Pateman's sexual presuppositions" and her denigration of "certain sexual activities," adding that this measurable increase in the consumption of fellatio porn between 1930 and 1960 "reflects a general change in sexual activity" (78–79). But none of what Bell states so casually in fact follows from Pateman's suggestion. Measurable change in sexual practices may be, and often clearly is, related to other things happening in the culture at hand. It does not follow from this that Pateman somehow disapproves of oral sex in general or thinks that fellatio, essentially and ahistorically speaking, is a misogynist practice. Bell's hasty jump to this conclusion simply reinforces what Mason-Grant calls "the conservative-versus-liberal framework of the sexuality debates." I follow Mason-Grant in seeking "a public discourse about sexuality that avoids repressive moralism while keeping open the possibility that sexual desire and pleasure, like hunger and pain, are always already infused with social, cultural, and political meaning, even in our bodily experiences of them" (122).

Perhaps the most literal example from today's Internet pornography market are the numerous rape porn sites showing narratives which directly reflect issues in U.S. foreign policy, such as narratives of American soldiers raping Iraqi women or Islamic terrorists raping American women, all of which is costumed and acted out.[2] Paul describes a recent film called *Gag Factor 15*, the fifteenth film in an award-winning series of films centered on the practice of deep-throating. In this installment, "the action takes place in a room full of men in head scarves and masks holding photos of torture from Abu Ghraib":

> Old school defenders of pornography may not be familiar with the direction in which Internet and DVD-era pornography has gone. . . . They probably haven't heard the soundtrack of such a film, in which one man screams nonsensically in what is supposed to be Arabic, while the other translates, "We will do to your women what you have done to our men—you degraded our people, now we'll degrade yours. The streets will spill over with spit!" They probably have not continued to watch as the film shows the men standing over a woman dressed in military clothes and dog tags shouting, "I was only following orders!" Or seen the penultimate move where one of the Arab men brandishes a sword and threatens to slice off the girl's head before the film's true climax, multiple oral sex scenes in which the girl is shown to choke on genitalia and semen. (2005, 8)

What Bell calls "desire" is neither an ahistorical force of nature
nor an unpredictable and unfettered maverick in the machine of
cultural production, but relates directly and often quite predictably to events in the world and their shaping of fantasies of gender, race, class, nation—all the axes of difference along which
power is unequally distributed. Thematizing this connection and
suggesting that this imagery is not neutral does not commit one to
a sexual conservatism which "disapproves" of certain sexual practices. Relatedly, Ensler's article on the Congolese hospital that
tends to the injuries of women raped by militia soldiers states that
the overwhelming majority of the injuries are fistulae—perforated
colons and vaginas—from being penetrated by guns, sticks, and
other weapons. This is not just systemic rape but systemic rape
that consists of particular sexual practices that signify in particular
ways at particular world-historical moments. Arguably, one of the
tasks of feminist inquiry, and especially of a feminist inquiry into
pornography, is to examine such significations in their particular-
ity rather than subsuming them under the blanket category of
dark and illegible "desire."

My attempt to revitalize MacKinnon's commitment to the
political force of figuring women as victims has nothing to do
with the "correct" way to read her, much less with the correctness
of the claim that all women are victims. She, Dworkin, Pateman,
as well as Sheila Jeffries and others, are certainly readable as sexual
conservatives, but this need not concern us. Furthermore, I agree
completely with Butler's critique of MacKinnon's critique of pornography on the grounds that the model of language MacKinnon
assumes in order to identify pornography as hate speech which
shuts down the speech of women is a Habermasian, consensus-
based model of linguistic community. Butler asks,

> But what might guarantee a communicative situation in which no
> one's speech disables or silences another's speech in this way? This
> seems to be the very project in which Habermas and others are
> engaged—and effort to devise a communicative speech situation in

which speech acts are grounded in consensus where no speech act is permissible that performatively refutes another's ability to consent through speech. (1997, 86)

Such a speech situation is problematic for Butler because it decides in advance the question of the "we" that politics must always be in the process of reopening. Her question, "what constitutes the community that might qualify as the legitimate community and debates and agrees upon this universality?" is a question the Habermasian model forecloses (90). My interest is in other ways that MacKinnon is also readable, the usefulness of her texts, their instrumental value and proper place in a feminist critical "tool-box" in the project of examining the consumption of Internet porn as a practice occurring within a determinable political and historical context.

For example, reading abjectitude/victimhood in MacKinnon's work as more strategic/ontological than empirical allows for a response to Amy Allen's (2001) critique of the concept of power assumed in MacKinnon and Dworkin's critique of pornography. Allen writes,

First, MacKinnon and Dworkin's conception of power is reductive. Not only does it reduce all power relations to relations of domination and subordination, which is evident from the way the term "power" is used interchangeably with terms like "domination" and "degradation," it further reduces relations of domination and subordination to a set of dyadic, master/subject relations. . . . Second, the claim that men are powerful and women powerless as such implies that women are solely (innocent) victims and men solely (guilty) masters. This is inadequate for a couple of reasons. First, it ignores the ways that some women are in a position of dominance and the ways in which some men are sub-ordinated on the basis of race, class, and sexuality. (515)

The second objection is immediately problematic, since MacKinnon and Dworkin's position in no way commits them to the idea that women cannot be in positions of dominance, even over men. In those cases, however, it is precisely the race, class, or sexuality of those women that places them "above" the others, and not their gender. In other words, for MacKinnon and Dworkin, women can be powerful as white, wealthy, straight, but not as women. Allen's first objection is further-reaching, namely the point that power is not best conceived as domination or as dyadic. On my reading of MacKinnon, however, hers is not a theory of power at all. Allen is correct to refer to this conception of power as "implicit" in these writings, since it is precisely never spelled out or argued for. On the contrary, the nature of power is never in question in this work, which focuses on the effects of "domination" and "degradation," asking the important question, *What kind of social subjectivity does sexual degradation produce?* Even if MacKinnon and Dworkin are fundamentally wrong that heterosexuality subjugates women in all contexts and at all times, I would argue that this question continues to be important.

This brings me to Allen's final critique of this conception of power, that "the depiction of women as victims also threatens to undercut the very aim of feminism: the empowerment of women" (515). As we have seen, if Butler is correct then the unthinkability of women's agency is not an obstacle to the agency itself. It forces us to begin again, to reinvent the human, but this reinvention is precisely that on which every political project depends. From this perspective, what Allen calls "MacKinnon and Dworkin's inability to conceptualize women's empowerment" is a necessary and critical stage in the process.

THE FEMININE INHUMAN

The scale on which MacKinnon attempts to critique the international human rights system requires abjectitude as a category of analysis. Her position requires that "limit" cases, the ones that cause breakdowns in intelligibility, move from the margins to the center of the debate. Thus, everything in MacKinnon's work that should appear strange and objectionable from, for instance, Bell's perspective, appears methodologically necessary, like the idea that "prostitution is the central metaphor for female sexuality" or that female sexuality is so exhaustively shaped by heterosexist norms that "we have no idea of what female sexuality is" (Bell 1994, 80, 83). Neither of these notions would seem strange in the least if it appeared in Butler's text, with its emphasis on unintelligibility and not-yet-subjectivity. From this conceptual priority given to feminized women, it need not necessarily follow that MacKinnon "assumes a unitary women's experience" or that she "reproduces the hegemonic discourse and system she is critiquing" (Bell, 85). Instead, I propose, the critique of hegemony that Bell is after, and postmodernism's "commitment to a multiplicity of difference" which conditions the possibility of intervention, depend on our explorations of the unintelligible, the abject, and the limit (187).

If we take seriously the political role of the abject woman as the conceptual limit of the human, it is the "positive" images of sex workers in texts by proporn feminists like Sprinkle and Hartley that become problematic, first epistemologically and then politically. In their contents, these feminist sex worker interventions reanimate premodern models of the prostitute body which figure it as sacred, healing, and magical, presumably in response to the way in which it has been figured, by conservative and antiporn feminist discourses alike, as coerced, impoverished, corrupt, and diseased. According to Bell, viewers witness "a reunification of the sacred and the obscene in the same female body" as prostitute art creates "a new social identity—the prostitute as sexual healer, goddess, teacher, political activist, and feminist—a new social identity which can trace its genealogy back to the ancient sacred prostitute" (137, 184). In response to traditions in which the prostitute body is silent, objectified, and degraded, these prostitute discourses offer a productive, discursive image of the sex worker.

To be fair, Bell's book provides readings of many different prostitute performance works, only some of which attempt to unite "the slut and goddess in all women," while others do the valuable work of destabilizing signifiers, disrupting visual expectations, and intervening in logics of identity (183). In fact, the very value of her work lies in presenting prostitute performances as an unexpectedly (to me, at least) diverse, mobile field. However, in her attempt to present these performances as inclusively and objectively as possible, letting them speak "for themselves," Bell fails to theorize her way through them. She presents them all as equally politically valuable. But it is of course possible (and even likely) that only some of these prostitute performances are instances of evental speech, whose figural force intervenes politically. And in fact, the two categories of prostitute speech into which Bell's analysis divides the individual projects are incommensurable. The labor of creating "positive" identities and that of intervening in identity politics cannot but work against each other.

For many proporn feminist activists, for example, the task is to undo the reduction of women to bodies, to animate the pornographic body so that it becomes a person rather than a mere body and enters the public/political sphere, participating in the creation of new social identities. For Butler, who remains continuously critical of identity politics, the place of the body in the public/ private distinction is quite complicated. "To be a body is to be given over to others," so that the body is precisely not the thing that stabilizes an identity. It is onto bodies that gender, sexuality, race, and all other social markers are inscribed from the outside, in ways the subject cannot control. The body as site of social signifiers functions as the condition of the possibility of sociality. "The body implies mortality, vulnerability, agency: the skin and the flesh expose us to the gaze of others but also to touch and to violence. . . . Given over from the start to the world of others, bearing their imprint, formed within the crucible of social life, the body is only later, and with some uncertainty, that to which I lay claim as my own" (2004b, 21). Because the body relates me, places me in relation to others, it is public first and only later becomes claimable as private and a site of autonomy.

To put it more generally, the claim that women are not "just" bodies hides an implicit assumption that bodies are "just" objects or things, thus reinscribing the age-old denigration of materiality and embodiment at work in the denigration of women. As Ann Cahill shows, the feminist critique of objectification in turn relies on an overly Kantian model of the person, which prioritizes the interior and marginalizes the body, failing to account for the role of materiality and embodiment in intersubjective relations and in ethics in general. Cahill's book *Overcoming Objectification* (2011) appropriates Irigaray's work in order to develop what Cahill calls a "carnal ethics." The new feminist task then is not to reject the idea that we are bodies but to let this do its work in transforming our conception of the social. I am interested in stretching this idea in a slightly different but related direction: the claim that bodies are

"just" things itself reinscribes the binary between animate subjectivities and their capacity to speak, and mute, inanimate matter
that poses a limit to that capacity, creating the necessity to speak
otherwise.

True matter *is* mute—bodies *are* things—and things, according
to Lyotard, are the condition of the possibility of the human.
Feminization, abjectitude, and the irreducibility of embodiment
are not reducible to the pure negativity of leaving women "outside" a certain conception of the social, but can function to transform that conception to one of sociality conceived relationally.
For Dworkin, the injunction to remember sexually assaulted
women is motivated by an ethics of inclusion, the position that
women, even those most feminized, "are people too," as the bum-
per sticker says. But Lyotard points to a different kind of remembering. He writes that the concept of international human rights
functions with the help of a systematic, deliberate forgetting of
the inhuman, of the fact that "in every mind and in the ensemble
of minds that is the republican community, there is something
that has no rights that needs to be affirmed, but that, beyond the
just and unjust, exceeds the mind of each and all" ([1993] 1997c,
193). Affirming the abjectitude or inhumanity of women does not
mean surrendering to the unjust material and ideological conditions that produce it. At stake is the articulation of a sort of limit
to the human that allows those who exist at or beyond this limit
to signify politically. The remembering of this "thing" which has
no rights, which is mute, stupid, opaque, inert allows for an
ontology of the political subject which prioritizes those who exist,
in a strong sense, outside of civil society, those whom the discursive and agential model of human rights has effectively excluded
this whole time.

Butler asks, "Can the exclusion from ontology itself become a
rallying point for resistance?" (2004a, 127). Rather than insisting
that Andrea Dworkin's exiled women have rights because they are
citizens of a global community, for instance, a political engagement

based on singularity and abjectitude affirms outside-ness and thing-hood not only as productive of the concept of humanity but as that thing which disrupts its machinery enough to allow for movement and new articulations. Lyotard's "thing" and Baudrillard's "object" both pose the same kind of intervention to a thinking of intersubjectivity-as-communicability and of the public sphere that forgets the mute, the immovable, the unrepresentable. A feminist affirmation of the thing, the object, the inhuman marks the very central place of women—or of feminized subjects in general—in the conversation about the ontology of the subject of rights. In Butler's words, "The necessity of keeping our notion of the human open to a future articulation is essential to the project of international human rights discourse and politics" (2004b, 36). It is because the condition of women at their most feminized radically poses a question to the very notion of the human—showing its contingency and vulnerability, its impossibility—that their situation as "women," not as "human," maintains the very instability and dynamism of the human that is necessary for change.

From this vantage point, we can begin to take numerous critical ideas seriously at the same time: Lyotard's claim that "rights and respect for rights are owed to us only because something in us exceeds every recognized right" ([1993] 1997b, 121); MacKinnon's commitment to prioritizing testimonies which "showcase" the most feminized women, and the claim that this must be at the forefront of feminist critique if we wish to counter the incoherent patriarchal logic of difference-and-equality (see ch. 3 of MacKinnon 1987); and a Foucauldian model of sex as the site where freedom becomes possible when sex becomes the site of limit experiences, or where experience resists intelligibility. In spite of the considerable differences between the ideological traditions in which American feminism and poststructuralism originate, the "radicalness" of Anglophone radical feminism may lie precisely in its attempts at breaking from its Enlightenment roots and gesturing towards something like Lyotard's inhuman "thing" or Butler's not-yet-subject all along. If

Butler is right, then Alfonsine's testimony about the unspeakable rape and violence she endured can function politically more effectively than any claim to her rightful belonging to the human race, precisely because it presents "woman" as a sort of conceptual limit to the legal model and philosophical conception of the human. And again it is important to note that the testimony may signify politically and not just ethically (by putting us in relation to another person and her suffering, for instance).

Returning to Kipnis's suggestion that the science fictional imagination is essentially subversive, it is in SF narratives that we find the most striking explorations of the limit of the human and images of the kind of inhuman that is significant for feminist concerns. The story that comes to mind immediately when we trouble the intersection between the inhuman, women, and feminism is *The Stepford Wives*, best known as the 1975 film, in which men living in a small, upper-middle-class town are secretly, mysteriously changing their human wives into nonhuman, "perfect" gynoid replicas that perform the functions of femininity unproblematically and without resistance. The irony in this story is that it is only by violent and artificial means that the feminine, which is supposed to come naturally to biological women, may be produced in patriarchal conditions. The protagonist, Joanna Eberhart, a real, human, imperfect, agential woman, loses her fierce battle with patriarchy and is eventually transformed into a Stepford wife. But this heavy-handed, binary contrast between human and inhuman reduces the inhuman to something like a programmable tool of the unjust system, while the human is about the triumph of the imperfect but spirited individual. This is not the imaginary of the inhuman in Lyotard and Butler—modes of being which trouble or even intervene in the legal and ontological concept of the human in fundamental ways. A study of inhuman social imaginaries shows that not every not-human is inhuman, and that the feminine and the inhuman intersect in subversive ways only under very specific conditions.

UNLIKELY HEROINES

A complex exploration of a femininity that plays with and riffs on its inhumanity is the character of Rheya in Stanislaw Lem's novel *Solaris*, made into a film by Andrei Tarkovsky in 1972 and remade by Steven Soderbergh in 2002. The story's protagonist, Kris Kelvin, is a psychologist sent to a distant space station on which scientists are supposed to be studying the mysterious planet Solaris. While on the station he experiences "visitations" by his wife, Rheya (Hari in the Tarkovsky film), who had committed suicide years before. Or rather, something not-human visits him in the form of Rheya, something at once fully formed and radically, heartbreakingly incomplete—without memories, history, or the slightest sense of personal boundaries. Rheya is a freak, unable to be in a room without Kelvin, completely dependent, pathetic, and simultaneously aware that she both is and is not herself, that she is draining him and yet can't bear for him to leave the room, that she both is and is not the woman he once loved. She demands to know—from him—exactly what she is. Her impossible, unthinkable mode of being becomes clear to Kelvin when he attempts to undress her and notices that there is no way to remove her dress. There are no zippers, ties, or buttons. She simply is, ready-made, without having come into being. She is sufficiently "like" the original Rheya, however, that Kelvin experiences a full spectrum of emotions towards her, from recognition, desire, and love, to disgust, mourning, and excruciating guilt. There are several gruesome scenes in which she "dies," including another suicide. But dying doesn't quite work in her case—she continues to return, much to her own despair, as long as Kelvin remains on the station. Towards the end of the story Kelvin in fact falls in love with the inhuman Rheya for her very inhumanity, and attempts to convince her that he loves her for "who she is" and not because she resembles his dead wife. She never fully believes him.

Rheya is not the only visitor on the station, but we hardly encounter the others, since they exist only in the private spaces, as embarrassing projections of the broken earthly psyches of the other scientists. In fact, we quickly discover that in the discipline of "solaristics," the scientists on the station had become obsolete—their funding cut, their work a public joke—because they had literally disappeared from the radars, unable to report on their activities or to explain to their superiors on Earth what was happening to them. They also refused to leave the station and return home. One of them has mysteriously committed suicide by the time Kelvin arrives. They do not function as scientists at all in the story but as the ultimate antiscientists, radically unable to give an account of the phenomenon in question.

The fact that Rheya's character happens to be feminine and beautiful makes it easy to forget that the very nature of the visitations is in itself hyperfeminine, apart from the genders of the visitors. The visitors both are and are not their hosts, thus holding their hosts hostage. Rheya's flights of panic, her utter dependency, the way that she appears to blossom precisely only when they are alone in his private room, making love and whispering promises, her helplessness even at the moment of suicide, at which she continuously both succeeds and fails—these are the markers of the feminine as "thing." She is radically vulnerable and exists only, painfully, "in relation" to him. In Tarkovsky's film's version, the one scene in which Hari (Rheya) appears the most sexualized, and in the most unspeakable, existential pain, is the one in which she fails to kill herself, which writer Geoff Dyer describes as "one of those sexualized fits (nipples prominently erect), of which Tarkovsky seems to have been fond, [the character] writhing away on the hard floor in a climax of abandonment" (2011, 112). At her least human, she is her most feminine. At her most feminine, she is her most abject, convulsing repetitively in a vain effort to turn away from the truth of her unmanageable materiality. If this is indeed an orgasmic moment, it is certainly not one of expression. Kristeva describes the experience of the subject's own abjectitude as follows:

If it be true that the abject simultaneously beseeches and pulverizes the subject, one can understand that it is experienced at the peak of its strength when that subject, weary of fruitless attempts to identify with something on the outside, finds the impossible within; when it finds that the impossible constitutes its very *being*, that it is none other than abject. The abjection of self would be the culminating form of that experience of the subject to which it is revealed that all its objects are based merely on the inaugural *loss* that laid the foundations of its own being. ([1980] 1982, 5)

Solaris ends without any conclusive, satisfying explanation of what the planet is or how it works, because the story is not really about the planet or about the fictional science of solaristics. Neither is it about Kelvin, whose character never really develops in response to these strange experiences. Despite the striking lack of women characters in the novel, it may be read as a story about gender, specifically about the vertigo of a femininity taken to its furthest degree. It is about the psyches of the men, isolated on the space station, their relation to abjectitude and their incapacity to turn away from it. If the men represent not only men but humanity, and the visitors represent not only inhumanity but femininity, *Solaris* is a story of the feminine thing as a conceptual limit to the human, as well as the breakdown to scientific and political epistemes in the face of this limit.

In Ridley Scott's 1976 film *Blade Runner*, the character of Rachel displays the connection between the inhuman and the feminine. "How can it not know what it is?" asks detective Rick Deckard after learning what Rachel herself does not know at the time of their meeting: that she is in fact a highly sophisticated android (called a Replicant) who has been programmed with another person's memories so as to appear human, even to herself. Deckard's job as a Blade Runner is to kill the renegade Replicants who have come to Earth from the off-world colonies in an effort to meet their "maker." When Rachel discovers the truth about herself, her love affair with Deckard begins, for reasons similar to the ones that make Rheya irresistible. She lives entirely in "Who am I?" mode, staring at Deckard with huge, pleading, watery eyes which implore him to help her even though there is nothing he can do for her. Of the three female Replicants in the story, Rachel is the least overtly sexualized, and yet Deckard's only response to her pain—and his urgency makes it seem like the only response possible—is to make love to her. She weeps in existential despair and he takes her to bed: throughout the film, it is this cycle that guarantees her femininity, linking it specifically to her inhumanity. The other female Replicants in the film, Zhora and Pris, are both inhuman also, but their femininity is incidental to this fact. Their sexual attractiveness is explicitly thematized in ways unconnected to their android status, even to their own awareness of it. It is only in Rachel's case that the limit of the human coincides with something like the eternal feminine.

The "Alien" film series contains yet another example of the inhuman as specifically feminine, namely in the fourth film in the series, *Alien Resurrection*. By this time, Ellen Ripley's character is reborn as a clone of herself, the eighth in a series of failed experiments by The Company to merge her human DNA with that of the alien queen. The film makes Ripley appear much more masculine than in any of the prior films in the series, dressed as she is in a sleeveless muscle shirt and easily holding her own with the human thugs who arrive on the ship, carrying hijacked human "cargo" which the scientists hope to use as hosts for alien gestation. In one scene, Johnner, a large, brutish man, begins to sexually intimidate Ripley as she practices basketball. She not only beats him at one-on-one but proceeds to beat him up in front of his uncouth friends. Her masculinity is further emphasized in the scenes with Call, a small and rather vulnerable female android character. In one of the film's most queer-inflected scenes, Call is shot, and Ripley sticks her fingers inside the bullet hole in Call's android body; as she slowly pulls out, her fingers are covered with white, milky fluid. In contrast to these displays of her (queer) masculinity, there is one scene in which Ripley appears spectacularly feminized, namely when she enters the room in which her seven failed clone predecessors are housed in vats. She finds the penultimate one, number seven, lying on a table naked, legs splayed open; a phallic machine is pointed at her abdomen in order to implant another alien queen inside her. In contrast to Ripley's tough, underground queerness, number seven is a victim of totalitarian, scientific-reproductive control by the establishment, a "real woman" in some sense. She may be used this way because her interests do not matter doubly— as a clone and as female. The conjunction of the inhuman and the feminine is thematized in this figure, who pleads with Ripley to kill her. We watch the anguish on Ripley's face as she very literally encounters her own "feminine side" and is faced with its inhumanity and abjectitude. She responds by setting number seven and the entire room on fire with a flamethrower.

All three characters have interesting and complex relationships to the normative, heterosexual narrative frame, as well as to the problem of death or survival. Rheya is unthinkable, so she must die; she wishes to die, but she cannot, because Kelvin's mind keeps bringing her back into existence. Both her death and her return are linked to the heteronormative narrative. As not-human, she must die, but as feminine and the object of Kelvin's obsessive, guilt-ridden love, she must return. Rachel's death is built into her Replicant constitution. All Replicants have a four-year life span but do not know how far along they are. She and Deckard run away together in a display of heterosexual love, which is supposed to conquer all limitations, including her mortality. And finally, Ripley's survival depends on her killing her feminized self so that no more alien queens will be implanted in clones of her. The only survival possible is the queer kind displayed in the final scenes by Ripley and Call, two ambiguously gendered nonhumans staring in wonder at Earth, where they have never been and which they must now somehow queerly repopulate.

Rather than pointing to the women in pornography and insisting that they are humans, too, perhaps there is value to examining all the ways in which the production of femininity in pornography troubles the limits of the human. I have argued that Internet pornography returns us to problems of speech and language, which means that the feminist insistence that the body not be written out of intersubjectivity and ethics at the very least requires the additional claim that the inhuman not be written out of language and politics. A politics which takes the event-in-language seriously but not in the sense of the speech paradigm, which as I have argued is in danger of falling into ecstasies of communication and community, requires a deeper exploration of the relationship between the feminine inhuman and the production of meaning. Kristeva indicates the central place of abjection in language formation:

> There is nothing like the abjection of self to show that all abjection is in fact recognition of the *want* on which any being, meaning, language, or desire is founded. One always passes too quickly over this word, "want," . . . but if one imagines (and imagine one must, for it is the working of imagination whose foundations are being laid here) the experience of *want* itself as logically preliminary to being and object—to the being of the object—then one understands that abjection, and even more so abjection of self, is its only signified. Its signifier, then, is none but literature. ([1980] 1982, 5)

The point is not that pornography should or even could depict the inhuman as I have explored it here. If we are calling for politically significant sexual transgression, however, and are hopeful that pornography could become the genre to speak it, then we must take seriously the possibility that Internet distribution functions to effect the forgetting (to borrow Lyotard's term) of the inhuman in various ways and on multiple levels, not in the contents of what is depicted but in the particular way that it forecloses the possibility of sexual speech to speak sexuality in figural rather than discursive ways.

8 PORNOGRAPHY, NORMS,

AND SEX EDUCATION

Both Lyotard and Butler are concerned with the question of what institutes conditions of sociality in the first place. Butler answers: the body. Lyotard answers: language. Both are concepts at the center of debates concerning pornography, precisely because the porno*graphic* is sexual speech, the simultaneity of representation and embodiment. Pornography not only represents bodies but affects them on many levels, sometimes very intensely. It acts on bodies by means of representations—in the more abstract sense of creating new bodily norms and ideals but also, and perhaps more interestingly, in the very concrete sense of signs provoking material, physical responses. The practice paradigm, in spite of its many strengths, misses this point. It misses everything about pornography that makes it irreducible to practice precisely because it functions as speech/signs/spectacle/simulacrum/representation. The practice paradigm has nothing to tell us about the semiotic aspect of porn, the relations between bodies and signs, the space between them. Kipnis holds that it is precisely this space between bodies and signs that creates the space for fantasy, which, she argues, "*is* a crucial political space" (1999, 203). I have argued that Internet distribution compromises the crucial political potential of the space for fantasy, or what I am calling the possibility of the event, or the potential of the inhuman to show itself inside or in terms of the pornographic.

"Perhaps when issues of pleasure, plenitude, and freedom are articulated more frequently in places other than fantasy genres like pornography they won't need to find their expression only in these coded and pornographic forms," Kipnis writes (203). In other words, when other forms speak these struggles in compelling ways, we might not find pornography so compelling—as consumers, critics, addicts, connoisseurs, activists, participants. But it may not be so easy to replace pornography with other discourses given that speech and sex are the keystones of modern debates concerning freedom. Both speech and sex are figured by cyberlibertarians in terms of autonomy, agency, and liberties to be protected, and correspondingly, both are imagined and figured differently in poststructuralist responses. Pace Kipnis, then, the question of the political belonging of pornography is fundamentally distinct from that of the political belonging of other forms of popular culture. That there is a special relationship between pornography and sociality is clear from the particular ways that porn troubles the basic infrastructure of modern political thought, as speech and embodiment are constantly pulled between "public" and "private" as well as between "normative" and "liberated."

Internet pornography raises the stakes of the debate around sex and speech in at least two ways. First, it reinvigorates the need to examine the speech paradigm and the society of communication. Second, due to the logic of the democratization of information, cyberporn gives rise to porn communities, threatening the role of privacy in the politics of sexuality in unprecedented ways. If we are following Lyotard, Baudrillard, and Butler, the results of these changes reverberate throughout contemporary discussions of political ontology, namely in how we conceive of both the body politic and, relatedly, the conditions for the possibility of resistance. What might those discussions glean from the inhuman Rheya? Or from the figure and testimony of Alfonsine? Or from the desperate eyes crushed into the silk bedspread of the rape victim in Ballard's fictional pornographic film? They are hardly feminist mascots of freedom or agency. And yet, in the political imaginary they might function to bring about the dehiscence Butler demands, precisely like the personal testimonies of women in MacKinnon and Dworkin's reports in the pornography hearings. These testimonies function on several levels simultaneously. The fact that the testimonies are personal functions on the level of ethics, demanding a relationship to an other, calling on us to witness a wrong, to hear a voice. The contents of the testimony, however, function politically in the attempt to represent something unrepresentable, the unthinkability of abjectitude. Not-yet-subjectivity cannot be unproblematically heard as "voice." This is what functions on the level of politics, interrogating the human, frustrating foreclosure, continuously reopening the question of the conditions of politicality itself.

PEDAGOGY AND SEXUAL LITERACY

I would like to conclude by indicating one concrete area in which the inhuman and the feminine rub up against each other in productive ways in the pornography debates. One significant change inaugurated by Internet distribution is unprecedented anxiety about the capacity of pornography to function didactically, to teach young people, especially young men, about sex. As long ago as 1999, a Time/CNN poll of teenagers stated that of the teenagers who had used the Internet (82%), almost half had seen X-rated content (Okrent 1999). If Kaminer is correct in her introduction to Strossen's book that the will to censor cyberporn is motivated by the fact that younger people invariably know their way around the new technologies better than their parents do, then the particular delivery system that is the Internet takes to a new level the worry that pornography provides a sexual education that is misogynistic, dissociative, objectifying, and otherwise morally and physically damaging. A British TV show called *Sex Education vs. Porn*, dedicated to this problem, aired briefly; British teenagers between fourteen and seventeen were surveyed about their pornography consumption and its effects on their sexual attitudes. "The average teenager, the survey suggests, claims to watch 90 minutes of pornography a week. Mobile phones and the Internet, despite supposed controls and content filters, make porn-sharing all too easy. Their viewing includes bestiality, group sex and lesbian intercourse. 'Porn,' says one boy, 'is everywhere.'"[1] But the problem for the creators of the show is not just that pornography is everywhere but that it actively misleads teenagers about what sexed bodies are like and what sexual practices really involve. "As well as the prospect of teenage boys watching violent porn, there is a concern about how it might distort their attitudes towards sex and women" (Apter 2010, 17). The teenagers surveyed and cited in recent pornography consumption research claim to prefer hairless female genitalia and surgically enhanced breasts. Many are having sex without learning proper contraception techniques because the pornography they watch does not show the use of contraceptives, or because "when boys see girls merely as sex objects, they're unlikely to respect them when it comes to matters such as contraception" (17). Paul's book has a whole chapter devoted to the effects of pornography on children, in which she assumes that it functions didactically and that this function is only enhanced by online distribution:

> Watching pornography, kids learn that women always want sex and that sex is divorced from relationships. They learn that men can have whomever they want and that women will respond the way men want them to. They learn that anal sex is the norm and instant female orgasm is to be expected. . . . Better to shape children's responses than to leave them to figure it out on their own. Looking for answers, they'll likely turn to the internet. (Paul 2005, 188, 190)

Multiple responses are possible at this juncture. One might respond that pornography does not function didactically any more than other cultural products do. In other words, if pornography teaches us about sex and gender in ways that are distorted, it is no different from other cultural products, many of which distort "reality" in various ways and may also function didactically. As Kipnis writes, "why presume that pornography alone, among the vast range of cultural forms, works as indoctrination, whereas every other popular genre is understood as inhabiting the realm of fiction, entertainment, even ideas, *not* as having megalomaniacal ambitions to transform the world into itself?" (201). A very different response comes from Mason-Grant, who argues that pornography functions didactically only using a very specific model of learning. The speech paradigm fails on the level of education, she writes, because it fails to "appreciate the difference between the force of ideas proposed and discussed explicitly and ideas tacitly lived out in our practices and backed by the normalizing force of social sanction" (2004, 152). For instance, she writes, it is possible to learn about date rape, the various forms it can take, and that it is a subordinating practice "without ever asking how one's own tacit judgment of what might count as consent during a sexual interaction has been shaped," or to believe that gays and lesbians deserve respect without examining how "one's own sexual practices and interactions are structured by and sustain heterosexism" (155). Pornography teaches on the level of practice, not ideas. She argues that in order to be effective, critical sexual pedagogy must itself take place on the level of practice rather than on the ideological level. Yet another response would be to point out that pornography centered on nonnormative sex could function as a desirable, feminist learning tool. For instance, what might be learned from those feminist porn sites which announce themselves as (at least in part) pedagogical, such as Nina.com, on which Hartley sells "instructional" sex videos teaching consumers how to engage in practices like anal sex, bondage, and group sex in more "responsible" (to whom?) ways?

As important as these objections are, I am interested in a different kind of question. Concerns about the nature of the sexual education that pornography might provide—whether it is bad (which might be said about mainstream straight pornography) or possibly even good (which might be said about some of the countercultural pornographies Williams champions in her work)—distract from what I think is the more interesting issue. If we assume that learning happens only under specific conditions and that, thus, not everything functions didactically, it is appropriate to ask whether Internet pornography is the sort of thing that can function didactically in the first place. Before we ask what it is that people are learning from Internet porn, we should examine whether or not it makes sense to say that what is taking place under conditions of pornography consumption is in fact "learning."

The texts which most express anxiety about children learning from pornography (1) fail to ask basic questions about what constitutes learning and (2) are underscored by different and incompatible philosophies of education. For instance, Paul assumes that learning is ideological (pornography shows sexually compliant women, so children learn that women are sexually compliant), while Mason-Grant assumes that repetition amounts to learning, like practicing a musical instrument. Hartley's instructional videos offer yet a different perspective. They themselves are not pornographic but explicitly teach how to have the sex one sees on her website, to faithfully reproduce the acts deliberately, not as an unintended effect of watching a video. Clearly, the three modes of learning represented here are not the same, and it may do more harm than good to continue to equivocate in this area. What is learning, anyway, and what is the political belonging of pedagogy? Is it simply an instrument of the state, what Foucault might call indoctrination into the episteme, a means of access to social power? Or is it instead the possibility of freedom, of thinking the unthought, resistance to norms? These questions must be posed if we take seriously Mason-Grant's argument that the only way to effectively intervene in pornographic practice is on the level of education, not the law (152).

For Lyotard, the inhuman is that part of experience that escapes the systems and institutions which render one "human," or fit to take part in the community of civilized humanity. "If humans are born human, as cats are born cats, . . . it would not be possible to educate them. That children have to be educated is a circumstance that only proceeds from the fact that they are not completely led by nature, not programmed. The institutions which constitute culture supplement this native lack" (Lyotard 1992, 3). The *infans* is that which does not speak. The role of education is to make the *infans* intelligible, to close the gap between humanity and inhumanity, to socialize and normalize the asocial, abnormal, mute, abject part. Lyotard argues that the model of literacy that trains us to use language as our tool to get ahead in the world, a tool in the service of power, is fundamentally mistaken about the relationship of the subject to language. We are not subjects prior to so-called language acquisition. Language is not a tool whose use we master, and ideas cannot be reduced to knowledge, understood as something to be appropriated and exchanged on some market (for instance, a "job market"). He describes a subjectivity *constituted by* language, transformed by it, continuously reopened, in the act of reading, to heterogeneity and the new. This constitutes real learning.[2]

If pornography in fact functions didactically, perhaps the more immediately worrisome issue is that education in the democratic state is in the service of oppressive, heterosexist norms rather than transgression and intervention. In other words, the problem might not be that pornography teaches violence or particular norms of grooming and gender presentation, but that it teaches conformity and subjection to social success rather than risk and invention. Were it possible for pornography to function didactically in the way Lyotard envisions, as somehow faithful to eventality and alterity, this would reopen the question of its pedagogical value. If, however, the ecstasy of community particular to Internet pornography precludes a true engagement with alterity and with the idea of language as that which inaugurates sociality, as I have argued, then Internet pornography offers nothing new, however ostensibly transgressive the practices it depicts.

Perhaps, then, the best we can do is the feminist pornography sites that function as normalizing, no more connected to freedom than the literacy education which teaches children to write just well enough to fill out a job application but no better, facilitating a certain level of social success at the price of a politics which would interrogate the conditions of politicality.[3] In other words, this sort of feminist pornographic pedagogy has its strategic uses and can play an important social role, especially in light of Mason-Grant's demand that sex education be focused not on ideas but on practices. But this remains a far cry from the claim that feminist pornography is operative in the production of "critical" (in Butler's sense) feminist sexual subjectivities, or anything like sexual freedom and the related notion of sexual responsibility, however they are both figured. Just as Lyotard argues that the democratic model of literacy education functions according to a misunderstanding of the relationship between subjectivity and language, it can be argued that pornography sites which profess to be feminist and to offer a degree of sexual education in the service of intervention function according to a misconception of the relationship between subjectivity and sexuality. Even if the Internet could yield a pornography that takes seriously the idea that sexuality could be critical, could such pornography function didactically at all? Is such a thing even possible under what we might call "pornographic conditions," the conditions of a sexual-political speech that is organized by and consumed as public, expressive, democratic? Or does the current epistemological and political climate render any other kind of sexual-political speech inaudible besides the normalizing kind?

ON TRANSGRESSION

The anxieties around pornography's didactic potential are related to the question of whether pornography is normalizing or transgressive. "The use of pornography is, I think, still widely regarded as a socially transgressive practice, despite its prevalence in contemporary society. . . . The use of pornography is thus distinguished from other media artifacts insofar as it is widely regarded and thus *experienced* as transgressive," writes Mason-Grant (126). Paul disagrees: "Today, pornography is so seamlessly integrated into popular culture that embarrassment or surreptitiousness is no longer part of the equation" (4). The difference between the two radically different assessments of the situation is that Paul is writing in the era of Internet pornography. How transgressive can pornography be when we discover on TV from our teenage sons that "porn is everywhere"? "How many eleven-year-old boys or girls would be ashamed or amazed to discover a copy of Penthouse or Hustler when the Internet regularly features full motion pornographic banner ads?" (Paul, 4). Paul and critics like her are right that thanks to Internet distribution, pornography use is no longer either regarded or experienced as transgressive. What their critiques miss, however, is that this is due not to its prevalence, or its popularization and accessibility in fact, but to its role in an ideology of popularization and accessibility, its central place in the logic of democratization. This is the "everywhere" that is politically troubling.

Might it be possible to create some separation between pornography and the Internet, or at least to produce pornography which troubles this relationship? Given what I have just said, this last suggestion comes not from some moralistic need to "save the children" from the dangers of the Internet but from the idea that in order for pornography to be transgressive, it must require actual transgression. Perhaps it should be more difficult to acquire, or even difficult to produce. Perhaps Sade could write his extraordinarily violent and strange sexual narratives only in conditions of revolution, under threat of prison, at the moment of the violent birth of modernity, when the rules of the democratic game were not just contestable but fiercely contested. Perhaps, on the other hand, pornography is what could transform the social meaning of the Internet from an instrument of democratization to one of transgression and risk. We hear this, for instance, in the fears voiced about viruses spread by porn sites. This fear shows pornography's potential to effect change—not in the transgressive nature of the sex acts depicted but in the considerable risks involved in the practice itself. The consumer risks damage to the very tool that connects him or her to the community. Suddenly, information becomes less immediate and available, and instead brings with it imaginaries of unwelcome invasion and contagion. What is clear in any case is that the existing feminist and/or queer pornography does not offer a sufficient antidote to the political effects of mainstream heterosexual cyberporn if we take seriously the idea that its "cyber"-ness is part of the problem. Perhaps instead of focusing on the production of new and different pornographies, feminist and queer interventions could devote their energies to guerilla tactics, such as ever better viruses attaching to mainstream pornography so that the Internet ends up associated with risk and exclusion rather than with the safety of community. None of what I am suggesting is likely to happen, of course, but my point is that, were it to happen, this would affect the social meaning of pornography.

The critique of popular media and pornography offered in the work of Baudrillard coupled with the critique of democracy in Lyotard and of sexuality in Butler together form a vision of Internet pornography as distinctly "American" and uncritical, foreclosing the political field. But these thinkers also give us resources for imagining what would have to be different for pornography to become a critically sexual practice. If we follow Baudrillard in his analysis of the centrality of female pleasure in the pornographic imaginary of continuity and sexual affluence, then perhaps this could change or be challenged in some way. If we follow Lyotard and Butler, it becomes important to be aware of the ways in which pornography forecloses the political, actively forgetting the inhuman and the event. It might be possible to produce a pornography that resists those tendencies, or to theorize the practice of pornography consumption in ways that convincingly make the case that it is possible to resist those tendencies in this practice.

To borrow a distinction from Lyotard, perhaps the problem is that today's pornographic pedagogy is about sexual expertise, not sexual philosophy. The expert "knows what he knows and what he does not," while the philosopher does not. Expertise is about increased performativity, efficiency, communicability, and ultimately, power. Philosophy is about suspending reality, patience, starting over. The expert speaks. The philosopher listens, even while speaking or writing. In contrast to the expert, who concludes, Lyotard tells us, the philosopher merely questions ([1979] 1997, xxv). Accordingly, then, some final questions. Can there be a philosophical pornography, one whose pedagogics incite sexual practices of questioning rather than increased performativity? If Kristeva is right that desire and abjection of self are two sides of the same coin, and that literature is the place that gives voice to this relation, can there be a pornography that is literary in this sense? I can think of no reason to answer no to these questions a priori, at least not in terms of the contents of pornography to come. The concern remains, however, that Internet distribution will continue to function in ways that foreclose these possibilities. This concern must be addressed as we attempt to answer content-related questions about the future of pornography and its growing spectrum of social effects.

NOTES

CHAPTER 1

1. See Dworkin (1997), especially "Pornography Happens" and "Race, Sex, and Speech in Amerika," both in *Life and Death*; and MacKinnon (1987) on the U.S. Constitution, especially her critique of American liberalism and the First Amendment in ch. 16.

2. See McGowan (2005), 23–27, for a thorough survey of attempts to define pornography.

CHAPTER 2

1. See McGowan (2005) for a survey of this literature.

2. See Merck (1992), 50–62, for a detailed account of how the notion of free speech signifies differently in the United Kingdom, where the legal code is not based on a Bill of Rights and no equivalent of the First Amendment exists.

3. See also "The Virtual Body in Cyberspace" in Balsamo (1996) for more extensive discussions of materiality and virtuality.

CHAPTER 3

1. Richard Lawson, "The Shrinking Boundaries of Being (A Certain Kind of) Twenty-Something," July 27, 2012, www.theatlantic wire.com/entertainment/2012/07/shrinking-boundaries-being -certain-kind-twentysomething/55077/ (accessed October 31, 2012).

2. For a discussion of the real in Gombrowicz's *Pornography* and other novels, see ch. 3 in Goddard (2010).

3. See "This Sex Which Is Not One" in Irigaray ([1977] 1985) for examples of her mimetic essentializing of the feminine.

CHAPTER 4

1. It is perhaps unfair to cite chatroulette here, since I am not sure whether it is a form of pornography or of what is called online sex. This raises the related question of the relationship between pornography and online sex. Just how distinct are they? If porn use may be considered a sexual practice, then could online sex be a form of porn use?

2. See Grebowicz (2010), *Humanimalia* *1*(2), for an analysis of the semiotics of gender in bestiality porn.

3. http://www.labour.org.uk/jedward-david-cameron-george-osborne

CHAPTER 5

1. Williams (2004), 2.

2. For feminist critiques of *Roe vs. Wade*, see MacKinnon (1987) and Poovey (1992).

3. www.isismedia.org (accessed October 25, 2012).

4. www.cnn.com/2009/LIVING/personal/07/24/0.women.watching.porn (accessed October 25, 2012).

5. http://tour.clubjenna.com/home/ (accessed October 25, 2012).

6. http://www.nina.com/journal (accessed October 25, 2012).

7. See my article in *Peace Review* for a more extensive commentary on this (Grebowicz 2008).

8. www.glamour.com/magazine/2007/08/rape-in-the-congo (accessed October 25, 2012).

CHAPTER 6

1. See also Butler's (1997) discussion of Kristeva's notion of the abject (133–34).

2. See www.raped-tube.com/movie/irak_rape_01.shtml and www.raped-tube.com/movie/islamic_rape.shtml for examples for this (accessed October 26, 2012).

CHAPTER 8

1. www.guardian.co.uk/society/joepublic/2009/mar/30/teenagers -porn-sex-education (accessed October 30, 2012).

2. For an analysis of Lyotard on literacy education, see my chapter in *SciFi in the Mind's Eye: Reading Science Through Science Fiction* (2007).

3. For a more extensive critique of the role of education in social success, see June Jordan, "Problems of Language in a Democratic State" in Jordan 2003.

BIBLIOGRAPHY

Ahmed, Sara. 1996. Beyond Humanism and Postmodernism: Theorizing a Feminist Practice. *Hypatia: A Journal of Feminist Philosophy* 11 (2): 71–93.

Allen, Amy. 2001. Pornography and Power. *Journal of Social Philosophy* 32 (4): 512–31.

American Convention on Human Rights (Article 11). n.d. http://
www.hrcr.org/docs/American_Convention/oashr4.html (accessed
October 14, 2012).

Apter, Terri. 2010. Internet Porn. *The Independent Magazine* (April
10): 16–19.

Ballard, J. G. 1996. *Cocaine Nights*. London: Harper Perennial.

Balsamo, Anne. 1996. *Technologies of the Gendered Body: Reading
Cyborg Women*. Durham, NC: Duke University Press.

Baudrillard, Jean. [1978] 2007. *In the Shadow of the Silent Majori-
ties*, trans. Paul Foss, John Johnston, Paul Patton, and Andrew
Berardini. Los Angeles: Semiotext(e).

———. [1979] 1990. *Seduction*, trans. Brian Singer. New York: St.
Martin's Press.

———. [1983] 1991. The Ecstasy of Communication. In *The Anti-
Aesthetic: Essays on Postmodern Culture*, ed. Hal Foster, trans.
John Johnston. Seattle: Bay Press.

———. [1986] 1999. *America*, trans. Chris Turner. London and New York: Verso.

———. 1987. USA 80's. In *Semiotext(e) USA*, ed. Sylvere Lotringer. New York: Autonomedia.

———. 1988. *Selected Writings*, ed. and trans. Mark Poster. Stanford, CA: Stanford University Press.

———. [1990] 2008. *Fatal Strategies*, trans. Phillippe Beichtman and W.G.J. Niesluchowski. Los Angeles: Semiotext(e).

———. [1997] 2007. *Fragments*, trans. Emily Agar. London and New York: Verso.

Bell, Shannon. 1994. *Reading, Writing, and Rewriting the Prostitute Body*. Bloomington: Indiana University Press.

Butler, Judith. 1997. *Excitable Speech: A Politics of the Performative*. New York: Routledge.

———. 2004a. Imitation and Gender Insubordination. In *The Judith Butler Reader*, ed. Sarah Salih and Judith Butler. Malden, MA: Blackwell.

———. 2004b. *Undoing Gender*. London and New York: Routledge.

Cahill, Ann. 2011. *Overcoming Objectification: A Carnal Ethics*. New York and London: Routledge.

Clapham, Andrew. 2007. *A Very Short Introduction to Human Rights*. Oxford, UK: Oxford University Press.

Cornell, Drucilla, ed. 2000. *Feminism and Pornography*. Oxford, UK: Oxford University Press.

Dworkin, Andrea. 1993. *Mercy*. New York: Thunder's Mouth Press.

———. 1995. Remember, Resist, Do Not Comply. First published by Massey College, University of Toronto, May 2, 1995. Reprinted from *Life and Death*. http://www.nostatusquo.com/ACLU/dworkin/remember.html (accessed October 14, 2012).

———. 1997. Race, Sex, and Speech in Amerika. In *Life and Death: Unapologetic Writings on the Continuing War Against Women*. New York: Free Press.

Dworkin, Andrea, and Catharine MacKinnon. 1983. The Anti-Pornography Civil Rights Ordinance. http://www.nostatusquo.com/ACLU/dworkin/other/ordinance/newday/AppD.htm (accessed October 14, 2012).

Dyer, Geoff. 2011. Into the Zone. *Paris Review* 198 (Fall): 101–41.

Ensler, Eve. 2007. Women Left for Dead—and the Man Who's Saving Them. *Glamour* (August). http://www.glamour.com/news/articles/2007/08/reallifedrama (accessed October 14, 2012).

Foucault, Michel. [1978] 1990. *The History of Sexuality, Volume 1 (An Introduction)*. London: Random House/Vintage Books.

Gallagher, Anne. 1997. Ending the Marginalization: Strategies for Incorporating Women into the United Nations Human Rights System. *Human Rights Quarterly* 19 (2): 283–333.

Gilbert, Harriet. 1992. So Long as It's Not Sex and Violence. In *Sex Exposed: Sexuality and the Pornography Debate*, ed. Lynne Segal and Mary McIntosh. London: Virago.

Goddard, Michael. 2010. *Gombrowicz, Polish Modernism, and the Subversion of Form*. West Lafayette, IN: Purdue University Press.

Godzich, Wlad. 1993. Reading Against Literacy. In *The Postmodern Explained*, by Jean-François Lyotard, trans. Wlad Godzich. Minneapolis: University of Minnesota Press.

Gombrowicz, Witold. 1978. *"Cosmos" and "Pornografia,"* trans. Eric Mosbacher and Alistair Hamilton. New York: Grove Press.

Grebowicz, Margret. 2007. Learning from Ender's Game: Childhood, Literacy, and War. In *Scifi in the Mind's Eye: Reading Science Through Science Fiction*, ed. Margret Grebowicz. Peru, IL: Open Court.

———. 2008. What's Glamorous About Human Rights? *Peace Review* 20 (1): 76–83.

———. 2010. When Species Meat: Confronting Bestiality Pornography. *Humanimalia* 1 (2): 1–17.

———. 2011. Pornography and Democracy: On Speech, Rights, Privacies, and Pleasures in Conflict. *Hypatia: A Journal of Feminist Philosophy* 26 (1): 150–65.

Hartley, Nina. 1997. In the Flesh: A Porn Star's Journey. In *Whores and Other Feminists*, ed. Jill Nagle. New York: Routledge.

Hayles, N. Katherine. 1999. *How We Became Posthuman*. Chicago: University of Chicago Press.

International Covenant on Civil and Political Rights (Article 17.1). 1966. http://www2.ohchr.org/english/law/ccpr.htm (accessed October 14, 2012).

Irigaray, Luce. [1977] 1985. *This Sex Which Is Not One*, trans. Catherine Porter. Ithaca, NY: Cornell University Press.

Ishay, Micheline. 2004. *The History of Human Rights*. Berkeley: University of California Press.

Jensen, Robert. 1998. Using Pornography. In *Pornography: The Production and Consumption of Inequality*, by Gail Dines, Robert Jensen, and Ann Russo. New York: Routledge.

———. 2007. *Getting Off: Pornography and the End of Masculinity*. Cambridge, MA: South End Press.

Jordan, June. 2003. Problems of Language in a Democratic State. In *Some of Us Did Not Die: New and Selected Essays*. New York: Basic Books.

Kipnis, Laura. 1999. *Bound and Gagged: Pornography and the Politics of Fantasy in America*. Durham, NC: Duke University Press.

Kristeva, Julia. [1980] 1982. *The Powers of Horror: An Essay on Abjection*, trans. Leon Ruidez. New York: Columbia University Press.

Lasar, Matthew. 1995. The Triumph of the Visual: Stages and Cycles in the Pornography Controversy from the McCarthy Era to the Present. *Journal of Policy History* 7 (2): 181–207.

LeGuin, Ursula K. 1993. Why Are Americans Afraid of Dragons? In *The Language of the Night: Essays on Fantasy and Science Fiction* by Ursula K. LeGuin. New York: Putnam.

Lem, Stanislaw. [1961] 1970. *Solaris*, trans. Joanna Kilmartin and Steve Cox. New York: Walker.

Lotringer, Sylvere, ed. 1987. *Semiotext(e) USA*. New York: Autonomedia.

Lyotard, Jean-François. [1979] 1997. *The Postmodern Condition*, trans. Geoff Bennington and Brian Massumi. Minneapolis: University of Minnesota Press.

———. 1992. *The Inhuman*, trans. Geoffrey Bennington and Rachel Bowlby. Stanford, CA: Stanford University Press.

———. 1993. The Other's Rights. In *On Human Rights: The Oxford Amnesty Lectures 1993*, ed. Stephen Shute and Susan Hurley. New York: Basic Books.

———. [1993] 1997a. Marie Goes to Japan. In *Postmodern Fables*, trans. Georges van Den Abbeele. Minneapolis: University of Minnesota Press.

———. [1993] 1997b. The General Line. In *Postmodern Fables*, trans. Georges van Den Abbeele. Minneapolis: University of Minnesota Press.

———. [1993] 1997c. Unbeknownst. In *Postmodern Fables*, trans. Georges van Den Abbeele. Minneapolis: University of Minnesota Press.

———. 2000. *The Confession of Augustine*, trans. Richard Beardsworth. Stanford, CA: Stanford University Press.

MacKinnon, Catharine. 1987. *Feminism Unmodified*. Cambridge, MA: Harvard University Press.

———. 1993a. Only Words. In *Feminism and Pornography*, ed. Drucilla Cornell. Oxford, UK: Oxford University Press.

———. 1993b. Crimes of War, Crimes of Peace. In *On Human Rights: The Oxford Amnesty Lectures 1993*, ed. Stephen Shute and Susan Hurley. New York: Basic Books.

Mason-Grant, Joan. 2004. *Pornography Embodied: From Speech to Sexual Practice*. Lanham, MD: Rowman and Littlefield.

McElroy, Wendy. 2004. A Feminist Defense of Pornography. Reprinted from *Free Inquiry Magazine* 17 (4). http://www.secularhumanism.org/library/fi/mcelroy_17_4.html (accessed October 14, 2012).

McGowan, Mary Kate. 2005. On Pornography, MacKinnon, Speech Acts and "False" Construction. *Hypatia: A Journal of Feminist Philosophy* 20 (3): 22–49.

Merck, Mandy. 1992. From Minneapolis to Westminster. In *Sex Exposed: Sexuality and the Pornography Debate*, ed. Lynne Segal and Mary McIntosh. London: Virago.

Okrent, D. 1999. Raising Our Kids Online. *Time* (May 10): 34–39.

Oksala, Johanna. 2005. *Foucault and Freedom*. Cambridge, UK: Cambridge University Press.

Pateman, Carole. 1988. *The Sexual Contract*. Stanford, CA: Stanford University Press.

Paul, Pamela. 2005. *Pornified*. New York: Henry Holt.

Peakman, Julie. 2003. *Mighty Lewd Books: The Development of Pornography in 18th Century England*. Basingstoke, UK: Palgrave Macmillan.

Poovey, Mary. 1992. The Abortion Question and the Death of Man. In *Feminists Theorize the Political*, ed. Judith Butler and Joan W. Scott. New York: Routledge.

Rancière, Jacques. 2004. Who Is the Subject of the Rights of Man? *South Atlantic Quarterly* 103 (2/3): 297–310.

Rubin, Gayle. 1992. Thinking Sex: Notes for a Radical Theory of the Politics of Sexuality. In *Pleasure and Danger: Exploring Female Sexuality*, ed. Carol Vance. London: Pandora.

Sade, Marquis de. 1990. *Justine, Philosophy in the Bedroom, and Other Writings*. New York: Grove Press.

———. 1993. *Juliette*. New York: Grove Press.

Saul, Jennifer. 2006. Pornography, Speech Acts and Context. *Proceedings of the Aristotelian Society* 106 (2): 227–46.

Scarlet the Harlot (blog). 2010 (January 16). This Sucks. www.scarlettheharlot.blogspot.com/search?updated-min=2010-01-01T00:00:00Z&updated-max=2011-01-01T00:00:00Z&max-results=27 (accessed October 14, 2012).

Segal, Lynne. 1994. *Straight Sex: Rethinking the Politics of Pleasure*. Berkeley: University of California Press.

Smart, Carol. 1992. Unquestionably a Moral Issue: Rhetorical Devices and Regulatory Imperatives. In *Sex Exposed: Sexuality and the Pornography Debate*, ed. Lynne Segal and Mary McIntosh. London: Virago.

Sofsky, Wolfgang. 2008. *Privacy: A Manifesto*, trans. Steven Rendall. Princeton, NJ: Princeton University Press.

Strossen, Nadine. 2000. *Defending Pornography: Free Speech, Sex, and the Fight for Women's Rights*. New York: NYU Press.

Sullivan, Andrew. 2008. Why I Blog. http://www.theatlantic.com/magazine/archive/2008/11/why-i-blog/7060/ (accessed October 14, 2012).

Sundahl, Deborah. n.d. "How to Female Ejaculate" (video). http://www.isismedia.org/female-ejaculate.htm (accessed October 31, 2012).

Vance, Carol. 1992. Negotiating Sex and Gender in the Attorney General's Commission Report on Pornography. In *Sex Exposed: Sexuality and the Pornography Debate*, ed. Lynne Segal and Mary McIntosh. London: Virago.

Williams, Linda. 1992. Pornographies On/Scene. In *Sex Exposed: Sexuality and the Pornography Debate*, ed. Lynne Segal and Mary McIntosh. London: Virago.

———, ed. 2004. *Porn Studies*. Durham, NC: Duke University Press.

Young, Iris Marion. 1990. *Justice and the Politics of Difference*. Princeton, NJ: Princeton University Press.

Printed and bound by CPI Group (UK) Ltd, Croydon, CR0 4YY

09/06/2025

14685884-0001